THIS BOOK IS DEDICATED TO STELLA RO.

Inspiring | Educating | Creating | Entertaining

Brimming with creative inspiration, how-to projects, and useful information to enrich your everyday life, Quarto Knows is a favorite destination for those pursuing their interests and passions. Visit our site and dig deeper with our books into your area of interest: Quarto Creates, Quarto Cooks, Quarto Homes, Quarto Lives, Quarto Drives, Quarto Explores, Quarto Gifts, or Quarto Kids.

First published in 2018 by Voyageur Press, an imprint of The Quarto Group, 100 Cummings Center, Suite 265D, Beverly, MA 01915 USA. T (978) 282-9590 F (978) 283-2742 www.QuartoKnows.com

Voyageur Press titles are also available at discount for retail, wholesale, promotional, and bulk purchase. For details, contact the Special Sales Manager by email at specialsales@quarto.com or by mail at The Quarto Group, Attn: Special Sales Manager, 100 Cummings Center, Suite 265D, Beverly, MA 01915 USA.

10 9 8 7 6 5 4

ISBN: 978-0-7603-6103-0

Digital edition published in 2018
eISBN: 978-0-7603-6104-7

Library of Congress Cataloging-in-Publication Data

Names: Kline, Gabriel, 1977–author.
Title: Amazing glaze : techniques, recipes, finishing, and firing / Gabriel
   Kline ; foreword by John Britt.
Description: Minneapolis, MN, USA : Quarto Publishing Group USA Inc., [2018]
   | Includes bibliographical references and index.
Identifiers: LCCN 2018020491| ISBN 9780760361030 (hard cover) | ISBN
   9780760361047 (digital edition)
Subjects: LCSH: Glazes. | Pottery craft.
Classification: LCC TT922 .K56 2018 | DDC 738.1/27—dc23
LC record available at https://lccn.loc.gov/2018020491

Acquiring Editor: Thom O'Hearn
Project Manager: Alyssa Lochner
Art Director: Cindy Samargia Laun
Cover and Interior Design: Laura Shaw Design
Photography: Tim Robison, except where otherwise noted
Technical Editor: John Britt

Printed in China

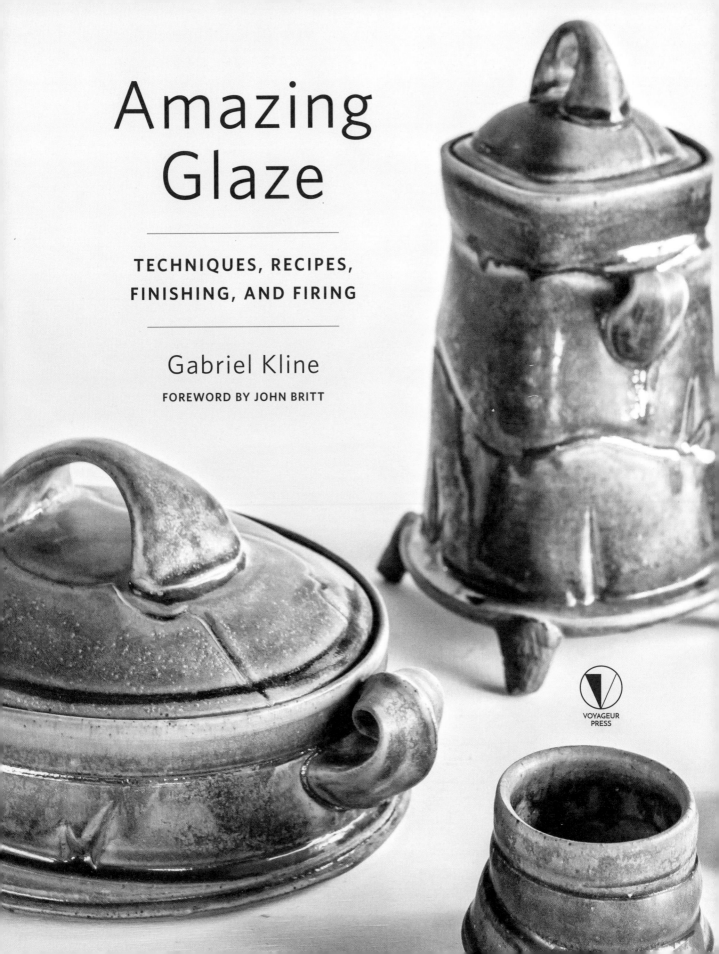

Amazing Glaze

TECHNIQUES, RECIPES, FINISHING, AND FIRING

Gabriel Kline

FOREWORD BY JOHN BRITT

VOYAGEUR
PRESS

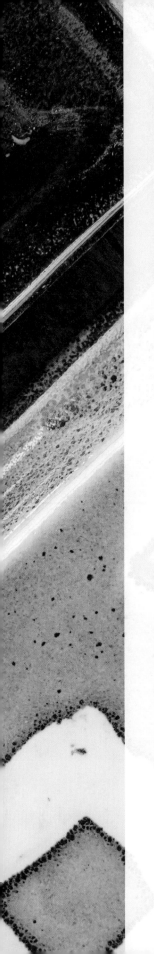

CONTENTS

Foreword by John Britt 6

Introduction 9

1. Get Ready to Glaze   10
The Glaze Kitchen   12
What Is Glaze?   21
Preparing to Glaze   27
Testing   32
Gallery   34

2. Applying Glaze (AKA the Dance)   38
Glaze Design: Forming a Plan   40
Basic Application
    (AKA Glaze Kitchen Choreography)   44
Single Coat   54
Layering Glazes   55
12 Tried-and-True
    Layering Combinations   56
Gallery   63

3. Going Further with Glaze   66
Building Depth   68
Resists   77
Alternative Application Techniques   85
Special Considerations   87
Gallery   91

4. Special Topics   96
Reds   98
Crystalline Glazes   100
Decals, China Paints, and Lusters   106
Non-Glaze Finishes   112
Raku and Atmospheric Firing   115
Gallery   125

5. Firing, Finishing, and Fixing   130
The Basics of Firing   132
Glaze Firing   136
Cleaning It Up   145
Testing Durability   150
Gallery   152

6. The Recipes   156
Notes   158
High-Fire Glazes   158
Mid-Range Glazes   170
Low-Fire Glazes   181
Raku Glazes   186
Slips   190
Underglazes, Washes, Terra Sigillatas,
    and Other Recipes   193

Resources   194
Acknowledgments   196
Index   197
About the Author   200

Featured Artists
Cayce Kolstad   42
Anja Bartels   82
Nick Moen and Genevieve Van Zandt   102
Julia Weber   110
Molly Morning-glory and Naim Cash   113
Josh Copus   119
Linda McFarling   122
Tisha Cook   138

FOREWORD

When I started in pottery more than thirty years ago, there wasn't a ton of glaze information out there. There were some classics, like Daniel Rhodes's *Clay and Glazes for the Potter,* Robin Hopper's *Ceramic Spectrum*, and Glenn Nelson's *Ceramics: A Potter's Handbook* (the text I used in college). There was also my main source for everything pottery-related: a dusty, worn-out collection of *Ceramics Monthly* magazines that dated back to 1954. These kept me pretty happy, providing countless tests to run in order to help me learn what was going on with my glazes. Still, I was always searching for new and better books to explain the mysteries of glazes. This included searching interlibrary loans to find whatever information there was out there, whether it was a dissertation on microfiche, an obscure out-of-print international book, or journals.

Today we have the opposite problem. There is an unlimited amount of information at our fingertips and that makes it hard to know where to begin—let alone to understand what information is most important. We are bombarded with beautiful images in books, in magazines, and on our phones of the most prized examples of ceramic masterpieces that have been collected over the course of thousands of years of human history, which we then want to reproduce in our kilns. So we find out the glaze name

and look for a recipe, but then we quickly find out that merely having a recipe is not enough information to replicate the deceptively complex glazing process.

It is a lot like wanting to make a spectacular birthday cake for a friend or family member. You search online among hundreds of recipes and come up with a beautiful picture of a cake you want to make. Imagine your surprise when you only get an ingredients list. There are no mixing instructions, no indication of the type of pan needed, if it should be greased, how hot to bake it or for how long, in what kind of oven, etc. It could take you a month of experimentation to figure out how to come up with anything close to a decent cake, let alone anything that resembles the beautiful cake that called to you.

This is the conundrum potters face; a recipe is only a list of ingredients. You need to know how to mix the ingredients; how to sieve; and if you should you dip, pour, paint, or spray it on. You need to know what temperature the piece should be bisque fired to; what type of clay is used; if there is an underglaze, slip, or terra sigillata needed; the density of the glaze slurry; how long to keep it in the glaze bucket to get the correct application thickness for the effect you want . . . and only then do you need to know how to fire it, which includes the cone, speed, and cooling necessary to achieve the results you want.

These are among the many techniques and considerations that Gabriel addresses in this book. He explains in detail the unspoken variables and how to control them. (For a prime example, see his discussion of density, starting on page 28.) Rather than just dunking your pot in a bucket for three seconds and expecting magic to happen, you can focus on how to achieve interesting surfaces. Gabriel lays out these methods so you can create an infinite variety of surfaces that are your own, rather than just copying and replicating images that inspire you.

We often think that if only we knew more about glaze chemistry and mastered the Unity Molecular Formula, we could design and create what we want. However, the real way potters find their own style is by working. You must pay attention, find something that speaks to you, and follow that direction to create something new. For example, Nick Moen's crystalline glaze (page 102) was not planned in a chemistry lab, but rather came out of the rush and tumble of making a living as a potter. This caused him to have to quick cool a load and that is where he found something very interesting indeed.

Gabriel has included a large, but curated, selection of glaze recipes to try out with a sampling of application and firing techniques, as well as plenty of inspirational images. He may not be able to solve the modern problem we have of selecting from endless combinations of glazes, slips, application methods, and firing cycles. However, his book provides a system for you to follow so you can find your own style and success.

Glaze on!

—JOHN BRITT
Author of *The Complete Guide to High-Fire Glazes*
and *The Complete Guide to Mid-Range Glazes*
johnbrittpottery.com

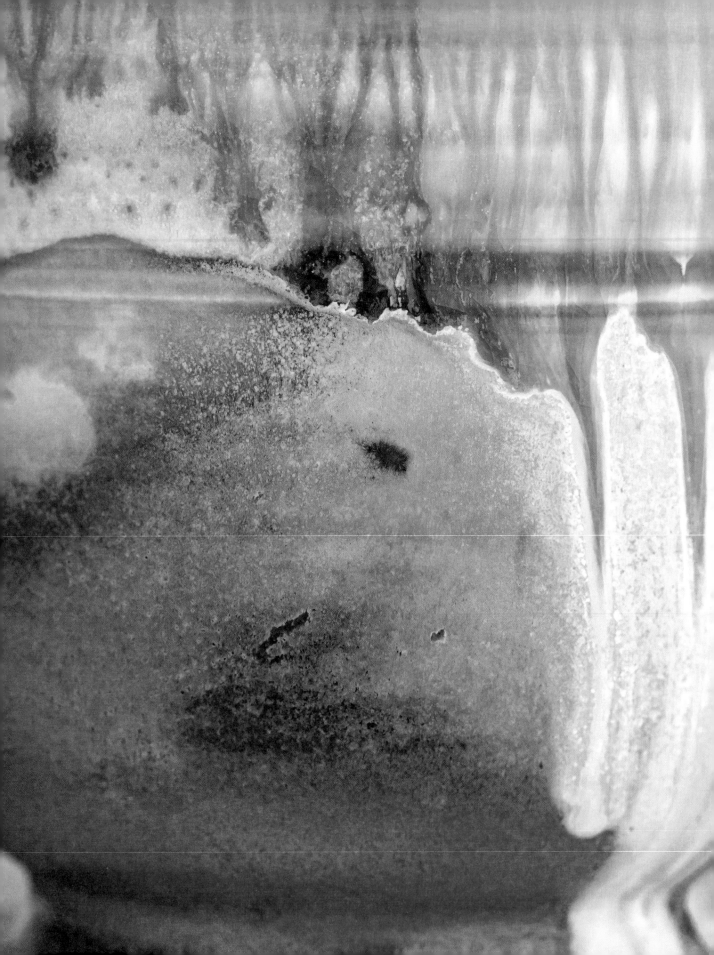

INTRODUCTION

For potters, opening a kiln is like witnessing magic. There's a moment when you can do no more than bask in the glittering, gleaming light of the pots on the top shelf, reflective with amazing glaze. After a good firing, we reveal the pieces in the kiln one by one, slowly, contemplating the subtleties and calling our friends over to take a look. As ceramic artists, we live for this moment. As humans, we're filled with joy when we create something beautiful.

On the other hand, a bad firing can ruin your day. The attempt to create something beautiful can seem a waste of time and effort when we fail. It leads to negativity as we question our competence, react with disgust, and use unprintable language to describe the results.

At Odyssey ClayWorks, in the mountains of Asheville, North Carolina, we have seen everything over the years—both the ecstasy and the agony. It has become our mission as an organization to eliminate as much of the latter as possible. We aim to equip our students with the information they need to make magic on a regular basis.

Amazing Glaze is the culmination of more than a decade of workshops, hundreds of classes, and thousands of firings. While it will serve as a great primer for those new to glazing, even the most experienced ceramic artist will find in it new techniques and recipes to try. In addition to providing the groundwork for setting up a successful glazing session, this book will investigate a bit of the chemistry behind the scenes (don't worry, you won't need a new degree), dispel many glazing myths, and profile several contemporary artists making waves in the field. Last but not least, you'll find a selection of curated, thoroughly tested recipes to try out in your studio.

Rather than seeing glaze as an afterthought to the "more enjoyable" process of working with wet clay, we'll seek to discover the hidden pleasures of the act itself. While many beginning potters focus on form—and there's nothing wrong with that—glaze is an important and necessary part of ceramic art. It is the way we dynamically enhance the surfaces of our work. It is my goal to dispel the myth that glazing isn't fun. Let's infuse the process with a sense of adventure, levity, and wonder!

By the end of this book, you will have the knowledge you need to create stunning, repeatable results that will wow the crowd and have your studio mates begging for the secrets to your success. I encourage you to be daring and adventurous in your exploration of the materials and processes. Take detailed notes, make sure to try something new in each kiln you fire, and share the results with your fellow potters. Seek to make work that adds to the field of ceramics. It is my pleasure to accompany you on this journey.

Happy glazing!

—GABRIEL KLINE

Glazing can be every bit as rewarding as working with wet clay! The glaze combination shown here is Tundra Sunset, found on page 61.

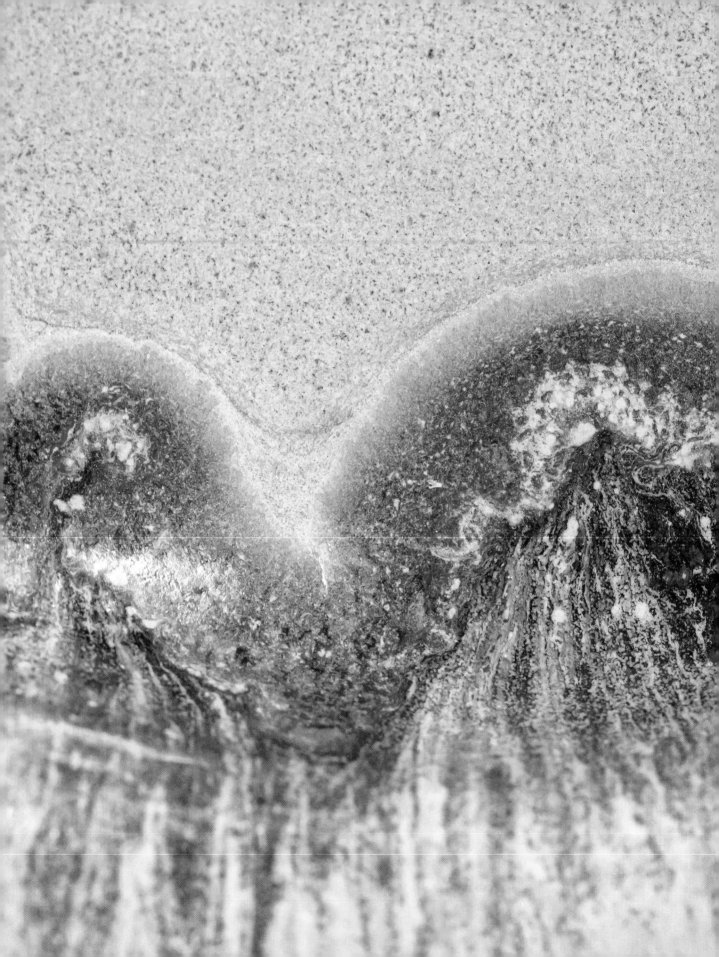

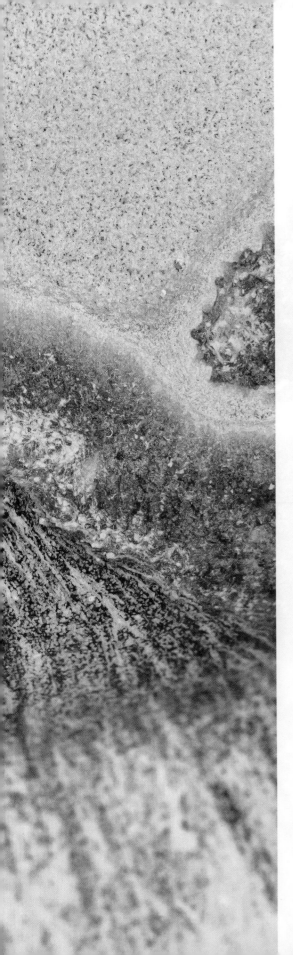

1

GET READY TO GLAZE

I often refer to the glaze area of our studio as "the glaze kitchen." While you should never bring food and drink into the glazing area, there's a good reason for the name. The glazing area in any studio should be set up much like a commercial kitchen. You want clear staging areas and a flow that lets multiple people work without getting in one another's way. The area should be designed with safety and efficiency in mind. In this chapter, we'll cover how to set up a glaze area so that your workflow can be natural, with a focus on safety and minimal physical strain. We'll also cover the tools necessary for glazing—and some fun extras!

Successful glazing also requires an understanding of what glaze is, how to work with glaze, and how to evaluate and test glazes. And of course, you'll need to know how to read a glaze recipe. While expert glazers may find themselves on familiar ground, I still encourage you to browse the next few pages, as you may pick up some ideas or spot some best practices even if you're a glazing veteran. It's surprising just how few of us come up in studios that use hydrometers (page 18), for example. For those of you just getting started on your glazing journey, this chapter is a must-read. Let's get cooking!

THE GLAZE KITCHEN

The very use of the word *kitchen* suggests that we are cooking something up. Indeed, let us think of the glazing process as preparing a visual feast on the surface of our work. In order to make glazing your work an enjoyable, easy, and efficient process, take measures to set up a glaze kitchen that reflects the natural flow of the glazing process. Just as a skilled chef moves gracefully and with no wasted motion in the kitchen, so too shall we learn to dance with our materials in the glaze kitchen. And while it may at first feel as if you have two left feet, you will soon be pirouetting your way to the kilns. (Think Fred Astaire and Ginger Rogers.)

SAFETY AND CONSCIOUS USE OF MATERIALS

Glaze myth #447: The creation of ceramic art has low impact on the environment.

Although potters and other ceramic artists have a reputation for being rather granola—that is, ecologically conscious hippies who love to play with earth—it is important to acknowledge that we are the original industrialists. For thousands of years, clay artists have mined raw materials from the earth, consumed other natural resources (including coal, natural gas, wood, and oil) to fire them, and released toxic chemicals, including carbon monoxide, in the process. I mention this not to dissuade you from working with clay, but to reframe the perception of the craft to acknowledge its environmental impact. When we begin to think in this way, our work becomes more ecologically conscious, focusing on responsible use of the materials and offsetting our consumption in other ways. There are many carbon offset programs that you can consider, such as Terra-Pass, which allows you to calculate the carbon footprint of your work with clay and donate funds accordingly to reduce greenhouse gases. I would like to encourage all ceramic artists to plant some trees, one way or another, at some point in their journey.

While it may seem somewhat of a buzzkill, it is vitally important to realize that in addition to the environmental impact of ceramic arts, many ceramic materials used in the glazing process can be dangerous to your health. Many are carcinogenic or otherwise dangerous with long-term exposure—including silica, which is present in all clay and glaze. Some are soluble (able to be dissolved in water and absorbed through the skin), and many, such as barium

carbonate, are poisonous. Just 5 grams of barium carbonate is a lethal dose in humans.

However, you can use glaze materials safely with the following precautions:

- Always use an Occupational Safety and Health Administration (OSHA)–approved dust mask or respirator when you are measuring, transporting, or mixing dry materials.

- Avoid submerging your hand in glaze without wearing a latex or rubber glove. Many materials are soluble and can be absorbed through your skin.

- Store all dry materials in lidded containers. A gust of wind from an open door or even a fan in the studio can contaminate the air with harmful material.

- Immediately clean up any spills or splashes with water. To avoid creating a dust cloud, do not sweep up dry materials. Do not eat or smoke when handling these materials.

DEALING WITH WASTE

When you are cleaning up spills, washing tools, or rinsing off a glazed piece, it's tempting to dump waste glaze material down the sink and forget about it. In most cases, at some point down the line, those materials end up in rivers and streams and the water table. Some of these repositories may be sources of drinking water in your area, and removal would require additional energy on the part of the water treatment plant. My recommendation is to install (or to encourage your studio to install) a custom trap below the sinks to catch as much of this material as possible. As you can see, the trap is a large metal basin on wheels with a drainage pipe at the top. Waste material settles

---

Organizing glaze ingredients and using lidded containers are both key to safety in the glaze kitchen.

The traps beneath our studio sinks help catch waste materials that would otherwise go down the drain.

at the bottom of the trap and can be periodically collected. There are a few possibilities for its disposal:

- Sieve the material through an 80-mesh screen and use it as a mystery glaze. The chemical composition of the glaze will be unknown, and will vary from cleaning to cleaning, but you just might end up with a glaze never before seen. It's worth a test before resorting to other options. This is our preferred method at Odyssey ClayWorks.

- You can fire the waste materials in a crucible in the kiln. To do this, you will need a thick-walled, high-fire clay canister. Fill it to one-third below the rim and fire to the glaze materials' maturing temperature. This will render the materials inert.

- The last option is the municipal landfill, but this disposal methods risks runoff and reintroduction of the materials to the water table or surface water.

Glaze taxis make it much easier to move large buckets of glaze around the studio.

INTENTIONAL DESIGN FOR MAXIMUM EFFICIENCY

When you are designing your glaze kitchen, you may want to sketch it out first using an aerial view, as you would see in an architect's blueprint. Measure your space and draw a scaled-down plan that you can fill in. You will want space for a large worktable, room for your buckets and tools, and an area for dry material storage. Ideally the glaze kitchen will be separate from where you make your work, but it is possible to convert your clay workspace into your glaze kitchen. In my first studio, I worked out of the basement carport of my house. Once I had installed shelving, my kiln, and two wheels, there was no additional room for a separate glaze kitchen. So, I would set large bats on my wheel and on buckets to create a series of glazing stations. This worked well for a long time, and I could produce lovely work in

an unheated basement with no running water. Even if your situation is not ideal, you can still produce ceramic gems in it.

Major considerations for the glaze kitchen include proximity and transportation to the kilns, access to water, worktables at appropriate heights, and drainage. If your glazing area has a smooth path to the kilns, a solid ware cart with good-quality casters can save you dozens of trips to the kiln. Some carts are commercially made especially for ceramics, but I have found that baker's carts also work well and can often be found used at restaurant supply stores. If your kiln is far away from your workspace, or if you work at home and fire elsewhere, plastic bins filled with bubble wrap or old blankets can protect your ware during the trips. I have always been impressed with Josh Copus, a local wood-fire potter, whose studio is in Asheville. He uses the blanket technique to drive his greenware twenty miles on country roads to his wood kiln in Madison County. He first places his greenware pots on ware boards, then loads the ware boards directly into the back of his pickup truck. He drapes thick blankets on top of the ware to cushion and hold the pieces in place. This creates a surprisingly successful bracing system for the delicate pots; he experiences minimal loss, despite the long trip.

Note: Access to running water is helpful, not only to mix glazes and adjust consistency, but also for cleanup. If your studio doesn't have running water, filling a 5-gallon bucket with clean water serves the same purpose and can act as your sink. Before the advent of modern plumbing, a trip to the river or well was a necessary part of the daily routine of every pottery workshop. Make sure you have a good supply of clean water at the beginning of every glazing session. At the end of a session, thoroughly clean the work area with plenty of water.

I highly recommend worktables that allow you to glaze your work without bending over and putting strain on your back. Posture is extremely important for ceramic artists, who spend much of their time leaning over their work in one way or another. It is a good idea to stretch your back, arms, shoulders, and hamstrings before working. (For a good example of a prework stretching regimen, see Ben Carter's excellent book *Mastering the Potter's Wheel*. The exercises Ben recommends apply equally to wet work with clay and to glazing.) Additionally, you should store glaze buckets not on the floor but elevated on a table or bench if possible. Ideally you should elevate glaze buckets about 2 feet off the ground, and you can use glaze taxis—castered boards—to roll buckets across the floor rather than picking them up. Why bother with the casters? A 5-gallon bucket neatly holds a 10,000-gram (dry) batch of glaze. When you add water, the bucket can weigh up to 50 pounds. Lifting it from the floor to the table or from one spot to another can put undue stress on your back, especially since you'll often be moving or using more than one glaze at a time. Another easy way to transport glaze is to use a 1-gallon pitcher to transfer glaze from one container to another. It is quick, easy, and will save you a trip to the chiropractor!

Dry material storage is another important consideration when you are setting up a glaze kitchen. Many glaze materials are carcinogenic in their dry state. Dry materials should be stored in containers with lids, and you should always wear a dust mask when working with these materials. If you are in business, OSHA requires you to keep a safety data sheet (SDS) on the premises for any dry materials that you are using.

TOOLS AND MATERIALS

In glazing ceramic work, the right tool for the job makes all the difference. If the following list of tools seems long, keep in mind that you don't need all of these items right out of the gate, and your studio may supply many of the tools and materials as well. This section is more to familiarize you with the tools of the trade than to provide a shopping list.

Buckets and tubs (not shown) It is useful to have a variety of lidded buckets to store your glaze, as well as several extra empties that you can use when screening and sieving glaze. Buckets should be made from sturdy plastic. Avoid metal containers, as they can rust and introduce iron into a glaze, thereby affecting its color and flux. You can purchase buckets at most paint or home improvement stores, but I have found that many bakeries purchase their icing in 5-gallon buckets and will often give away the empties for free. What size buckets will you need? Let's look at some common batch sizes:

- 2,000 grams of glaze (dry) will fit neatly into a 1-gallon bucket.

- 5,000 grams of glaze will fit into a 3-gallon bucket.

- 10,000 grams of glaze will fit into a 5-gallon bucket.

- 20,000 grams of glaze will fit into a 10-gallon rubber trashcan.

- 100,000 grams of glaze will fit into a 55-gallon plastic drum.

Drills, whisks, and stir sticks Ⓐ Glazes need to be thoroughly mixed in order to perform effectively. Materials settle out, so all glazes should be stirred frequently to ensure the chemical integrity of the recipe. A stir stick works well, but it is the most time-consuming

option. A large whisk, available at restaurant supply stores, mixes glaze more quickly. However, due to its curved shape, it cannot reach into the corner of a bucket, where the bottom and side(s) meet. A drill with a blunger attachment (a long rod with spinning blades) is the quickest, most effective means of mixing a glaze, reaching the material in the corner of the bucket while quickly homogenizing the recipe.

Sieves Ⓑ Almost all glazes benefit from sieving. A sieve will get rid of any chunks of undissolved material in the glaze, which almost always cause problems, such as flaking off or creating a mottled surface. Sieves come in a number of different sizes, depending on application. Small sieves can be used for testing. A large Talisman screen utilizes an interchangeable screen and brushes attached to a rotary handle, which allows you to screen larger amounts of materials quickly without dipping your hand in the glaze. Note that sieves also have several different mesh sizes. Mesh size refers to the number of holes in the screen per square inch. An 80-mesh screen is usually sufficient, but some glazes will benefit from using a higher-number mesh. (A mesh with more holes per square inch screens a finer particle size.)

Tongs Ⓒ There are several types of glazing tongs. For vertical work, the red-handled stainless-steel tongs made by Kemper work well. For glazing flatware, such as plates and shallow bowls, use adjustable channel lock tongs. They hold the work at a different angle, allowing you to move the piece horizontally through the glaze, resulting in a smoother coat. Tongs will generally leave a "vampire bite" at the contact points, which you will need to fill in with a brush later. Tongs should be used only with smaller work, as the weight of the glaze inside a larger piece can put too much pressure on the contact points with the

tongs, causing the bisqueware to crack. For larger work, you may need to use your gloved hands.

Hydrometer Ⓓ A hydrometer is a glass tube filled at the bottom with lead, calibrated to measure specific gravity (SG), or the density of a liquid—in this case glaze—relative to water. A hydrometer is the fastest way to measure specific gravity, although there are several other options. See page 28 for an in-depth discussion of specific gravity and its importance in glazing.

Funnels Ⓔ Funnels are useful for channeling glaze into narrow-necked forms, filling up glaze trailers, and for calculating specific gravity. Funnels are also often used in conjunction with small screens when creating glaze trailers.

Pitchers Ⓕ It is nice to have a variety of pitchers available for pouring glaze over a piece and for transporting glaze from one container to another. A handle that's open-ended on the bottom allows you to hang the pitcher on the inside rim of a bucket between pours, preventing drips from forming a messy puddle of glaze outside of the bucket.

Banding wheels Ⓖ Banding wheels are often used for waxing round, symmetrical forms, but can also be used for glazing and decorating. Shimpo makes the best banding wheels. (That's an unsolicited endorsement, really!) While more expensive than some other options, they last a lifetime and have the smoothest rotation.

Brushes Ⓗ Keep a variety of brushes on hand for different applications, including wax resist, brushwork with glaze, and filling in those pesky vampire bites. Soft-bristled, floppy brushes hold wax and glaze more effectively than hard-bristled brushes do.

Sponges ① Sponges are an absolute necessity for cleaning up. In addition, you can also customize sponges and use them to apply glaze to a piece. Both synthetic and natural sponges work well in these capacities.

Respirator or dust mask ① Glaze materials in their dry form can be a health hazard if inhaled. You should wear an OSHA-certified dust mask or respirator at all times when working with these materials in their dry state and when spraying glaze. Be sure that the mask or respirator is certified for fine particles. The N100 class of dust masks and respirators is recommended for use with ceramic materials.

Gloves ⓚ If a piece is too large for dipping tongs, and requires submerging your hands in glaze, use latex or rubber gloves. Some glaze materials are soluble and can be absorbed through the skin.

Pebble bowls and bus tubs (not shown) Pebble bowls and bus tubs, available at any restaurant supply store, make great containers for glazing large or flat work that is too wide to easily fit into the glaze bucket.

Glaze trailers ⓛ Used to apply small amounts of glaze in specific areas, glaze trailers come in a variety of shapes and sizes. Condiment squeeze bottles, tjanting tools for batik, and hair dye applicators can all be repurposed as glaze trailers.

Diamond grinding disks, sanding sponges, and rotary tools (Dremel) attachments ⓜ These tools are designed to help remove unwanted glaze from pieces and to soften any rough edges. While traditional sandpaper and silicon carbide work well and are economical, diamond grinding disks, sanding sponges, and rotary tool attachments are long-lasting and do the work quicker. They are worth the investment. I wish I had discovered these tools earlier in my career. You can often find them at stores that supply glass blowers. Dremel tools are available at home improvement stores.

Spray guns ⓝ There are many different models of spray guns, some designed to use with paints. These high-volume, low pressure (HVLP) spray guns work equally well with glaze. The simplest version yields a conical spray, that is, one that results in a circular shape on the piece. Other guns are adjustable and can spray glaze in a vertical or horizontal oval. Spraying is just one method of applying glaze; you can find out more on page 52.

Spray booth (not shown) A spray booth provides an area to spray a glaze on your work while containing and venting the excess aerated glaze outdoors. Spray booths are commercially produced but can be custom-made with materials as simple as cardboard and a box fan.

Air compressor (not shown) Compressed air has several uses in glazing, including aerating glaze in the spray booth and cleaning bisque fired work of pinhole-producing dust. Your air compressor should be able to maintain 80 psi for cleaning bisque and 40 psi for spraying glaze.

Triaxial blend board ⓞ When you are testing out three glaze materials in relationship to one another, this board can help keep everything organized, neat, and tidy. The board itself comprises fifteen small containers in a triangular grid, with each corner of the triangle representing 100 percent of a given material. The interactions between these materials can be mapped in different, regular ratios, giving the user a sense of the way the materials will perform in proportion to one another.

WHAT IS GLAZE?

"Nice glaze" is something one potter might say to another, pointing to the surface of a pot. But just what is that glassy surface made of? Glaze begins its life as a combination of pulverized ingredients that have been slaked with water to create a slurry, which can then be applied to the surface of a ceramic piece through several different methods. When fired to the appropriate temperature, the glaze will melt, permeate the surface of the piece, and then cool in a solid state, creating a permanent coating or "skin" on the piece.

Glazing is not necessary for every piece you make, or even desirable in some applications. An unglazed piece may be fired, as in the case of terra cotta flowerpots, roofing tile, and some sculptures. (The clay is then referred to as "naked.") So why glaze your work? There are two very good reasons. First, by glazing you add visual interest to your pieces. Second, in the case of functional work, glaze creates the impermeable surface that allows your piece to be used with food and drink.

A BIT OF CHEMISTRY

If you've ever cracked open a glaze book or searched for a recipe online only to be overwhelmed with the idea of glaze chemistry, fear not. While the chemistry involved may seem intimidating, you can achieve terrific results without knowing a single thing about what is in a glaze. Additionally, the focus of this book is on the practical application of the glaze—that is, how to get just the right amount of glaze in the right spot. We won't go too far down the road of glaze chemistry.

That said, it is still important to have at least a basic understanding of the material in a glaze as early as possible in your ceramic journey. Knowing what makes a glaze is necessary if you want to be able to adjust a recipe, which will allow you to expand your palette exponentially.

Here's the crash course! Three main components compose a typical glaze, and each one is important in creating a glassy surface on your work: a glass-former, a stabilizer, and a flux. This combination is often referred to as a "base glaze."

- Glass-formers (silicon dioxide [SiO_2] and boron [B_2O_3]) provide durability.

- Stabilizers, sometimes referred to as "refractories," mainly alumina, sourced from kaolin (chemical compound $Al_2O_3 \cdot 2SiO_2$), help the glaze stay on the piece. Even the best glass-former won't do much good if it's running down the side of your pot.

- Fluxes (the group of oxides including lithium, sodium, magnesium, potassium, calcium, strontium, barium, zinc, and lead) ensure that the glaze melts at the appropriate temperature. You can have a great recipe when it comes to glass-formers and stabilizers, but without the right flux, it will not melt the way you want.

Please note that some ingredients listed in a glaze recipe may contain more than one of the groups of oxides, and that some, such as iron oxide, can perform multiple roles, acting as flux, stabilizer, and colorant. For example, Edgar Plastic Kaolin (EPK) contains glass-formers, stabilizers, and trace amounts of fluxes.

Understanding a few basics about glaze composition can help you predict how glazes will look when fired. The base glaze shown here is Spearmint, discussed on pages 22–24, with the recipe on page 178.

Chemical Analysis of EPK

SiO_2 ....45.73%

Al_2O_3.......................................37.36%

Fe_2O_3 ....0.79%

TiO_2 ....0.37%

P_2O_5 ....0.236%

CaO 0.18%

MgO 0.098%

Na_2O.......................................0.059%

K_2O 0.33%

Analysis courtesy of Edgar Plastic Kaolin

The ratio of glass-formers, stabilizers, and fluxes in relation to one another is known as the Seger (or Unity) formula. It is expressed with the total fluxes equaling 1, and the total glass-former and stabilizers expressed in ratio to the fluxes. This ratio can provide some insight into the relative degree of gloss of the glaze. If the glass-former to stabilizer ratio (SiO_2:Al_2O_3) is higher, than, say, 10:1, you will have a glossy glaze. A lower ratio of glass-former to stabilizer at 5:1 will be more matte. In this way, the Unity or Seger formula can provide insight into the properties of a glaze.

In addition to the materials found in the base glaze, many recipes will include several other materials that affect the way the glaze performs, both in terms of application and fired results. For example, these materials may be responsible for keeping the glaze suspended in water (such as Epsom salts), coloring the glaze (copper carbonate, rutile, and mason stains), or opacifying the glaze (Zircopax and Superpax).

If glaze chemistry floats your boat, several excellent books have been written with a strong focus on the subject. For a top-notch review of ceramic materials, I recommend John Britt's *Complete Guide to High-Fire Glazes* and *Complete Guide to Mid-Range Glazes* as well as Daniel Rhodes' *Clay and Glazes for the Potter*.

HOW TO READ A GLAZE RECIPE

Most glaze recipes will come in a standardized form. The base glaze materials will add up to 100 percent, with additives such as colorants, suspenders (materials that keep a glaze from settling out), and opacifiers listed separately. This means the sum of all ingredients may total more than 100 percent. (Note: The figures in the recipe may be read as percentages, or as units of measurement—grams, ounces, pounds.) No matter what category of measuring units you use, the recipe will remain intact as long as you stay consistent in using that same unit of measurement. For example, let's look at a glaze recipe for Spearmint:

Spearmint, Cone 6

Wollastonite	28.00%
EPK	28.00%
Ferro Frit 3195	23.00%
Silica	17.00%
Nepheline Syenite	4.00%
Total	**100.00%**

Also Add

Light Rutile	6.00%
Copper Carbonate	3.00%

Contained within these ingredients are the aforementioned groups of oxides required for a glaze: glass-formers, stabilizers, and fluxes, as well as the additional colorant groups. You may also see fluxes referred to as the RO/R_2O group, stabilizers as R_2O_3, and glass-formers as the RO_2 group.

In some cases, you may also see a chemical breakdown of the glaze expressed in the form of the Seger (Unity) formula, where the flux group will add up to 1.00, and the R_2O_3 (stabilizer) and RO_2 (glass-former) can be expressed in ratio to the fluxes. You'll see the ratio of glass-formers to stabilizers is 6.94:1, suggesting a low-gloss glaze, but not matte.

Chemical Formula for Spearmint, Cone 6

RO/R$_2$O (FLUX)

0.01	K$_2$O (Potassium Oxide)
0.09	Na$_2$O (Sodium Oxide)
0.90	CaO (Calcium Oxide)
1.00	**Total fluxes**

R$_2$O$_3$ (STABILIZER)

0.4	Al$_2$O$_3$ (Aluminum Oxide)
0.4	**Total stabilizers**

RO$_2$ (GLASS-FORMERS)

3.00	SiO$_2$ (Silicon Dioxide)
3.00	**Total glass-formers**

OTHER

0.02	Fe$_2$O$_3$ (Iron Oxide)
0.10	CuO (Copper Oxide)
0.22	TiO$_2$ (Titanium Dioxide)
0.23	B$_2$O$_3$ (Boron Oxide)
0.57	**Total other ingredients**

RATIO OF GLASS FORMERS TO STABILIZERS:

6.94:1

ADJUSTING GLAZE RECIPES

"Tweaking" a glaze, also known as adjusting a glaze recipe, combines art and science. Depending on the desired characteristics of a glaze (more or less shiny, more or less matte, more or less runny, more or less intense color, a different color altogether), you may employ different strategies. Varying the amount of glass-formers, stabilizers, and fluxes will affect the base glaze. Adding more glass-formers will result in a glossier glaze. More stabilizers will make it increasingly matte. More flux will cause it to melt and eventually run. Varying the amount of coloring oxides or mason stains will change its color. It is even possible to adjust a cone 10 glaze to fire at cone 6 by adding more flux, and to adjust in the opposite direction by adding more stabilizers. As a result of these tweaks, your base glaze may no longer add up to 100 percent. Thus, you will occasionally find tweaked recipes that do not add up to 100 percent. If you want to retotal the glaze to add up to 100 percent, divide each ingredient by the total and multiply by 100. For example:

Ingredient A	80%
Ingredient B	20%
Ingredient C	15%
Total	115%

Then:

Ingredient A

$80 \div 115 = 0.6956 \times 100 = 69.56\%$

Round to 70%

Ingredient B

$20 \div 115 = 0.1739 \times 100 = 17.39\%$

Round to 17%

Ingredient C

$15 \div 115 = 0.1304 \times 100 = 13.04\%$

Round to 13%

Total	100%

ADJUSTING BATCH SIZE

You may need to adjust your batch size to suit your needs. To do this, take the original recipe and decide how large you want to make it. A 5,000-gram batch of a base glaze, for example, will fit neatly in a 3-gallon bucket. To get from 100 units to 5,000, multiply each ingredient by 50. By extension, if you were going to make a 10,000-gram batch, you would multiply each ingredient by 100. Using Spearmint as our example, the math would be as follows for a 5,000-gram batch. (Note that the coloring oxides Light Rutile and Copper Carbonate are additions to the base glaze recipe, and the end recipe with colorants will weigh 5,450 grams.)

Spearmint, Cone 6

Wollastonite ....28.00 × 50 = 1400.00
EPK.............................28.00 × 50 = 1400.00
Ferro Frit 3195 ....23.00 × 50 = 1150.00
Silica ....17.00 × 50 = 850.00
Nepheline Syenite ......4.00 × 50 = 200.00
Total (base glaze)....... **100.00 × 50 = 5000.00**

Also Add

Light Rutile ....6.00 × 50 = 300.00
Copper Carbonate.......3.00 × 50 = 150.00
Total .... **109.00 × 50 = 5450.00**

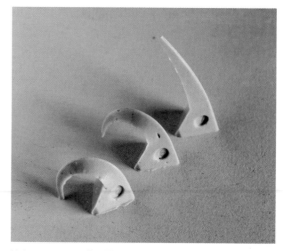

Using a cone pack will give you the most reliable data on your firing.

CONES, TEMPERATURE, AND HEAT WORK

Cones are small pyramids of compressed ceramic material that have been formulated to melt at a specific temperature in relation to the rate of climb. Cones indicate the maturing of clay and glazes. Cones are enormously helpful to the ceramic artist, as they provide a visual confirmation of what has happened (or is happening) inside the kiln. There are different types of cones, including small cones, large cones, and self-supporting cones. Small cones are often used in kilns that have a kiln sitter, a device that automatically shuts off the kiln. The small cone is placed horizontally in the kiln sitter, with the shut off bar resting on top of the cone. The bar, when in the up position, allows the kiln to continue firing. When the cone melts, the bar falls, the electrical circuit is disconnected, and the kiln shuts off.

Large cones cannot be used in a kiln sitter. They need some kind of support to hold them up. Self-supporting cones are similar in size to large cones, but can stand alone, which saves time over the long run. Large cones and self-supporting cones should be placed in front of the spyholes of the kiln. They are referred to as "witness cones." When several cones are used in this way, the group is referred to as a "cone pack." A cone pack usually comprises a guide cone, guard cone, and target cone. Even if your kiln has a thermocouple and computerized controller, these can be slightly miscalibrated or eventually wear out. As a rule, always fire to a witness cone, rather than relying on the controller and thermocouple.

A large cone is mature when the tip of the cone bends over and touches the shelf. A self-supporting cone is mature when its tip is parallel with the base of the pyramid that supports the cone, not when the tip hits the shelf. This is a common mistake. This visual illustrates self-supporting cones that are underfired, on target, and overfired, respectively.

Glaze myth #214: Cones measure the temperature inside the kiln.

Actually, cones measure temperature *and* time. For your glazes to perform properly—that is, to achieve the appropriate degree of melt and coloration—they must undergo a certain amount of heat work, which is a function of both temperature and time. Like to bake? We can use brownies as a helpful analogy to illustrate the effect of heatwork. Brownies baked at

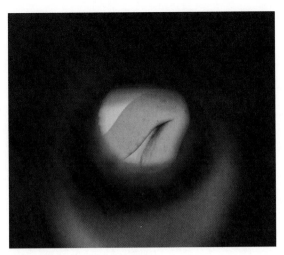
A witness cone during a firing.

400 degrees for 20 minutes will be moist and fudgy, while brownies baked at the same temperature for 40 minutes will be crispy. It is not just the maximum temperature achieved, but how long it takes to get there and how long the temperature is held that will also affect the end result. Similarly, if we fire quickly, the cone will bend at a higher temperature. In a medium fire, the cone will melt at a slightly lower temperature, as the glaze has experienced more heat work. In a slow firing, the cone will melt at an even lower firing temperature.

KILN ATMOSPHERE
(OXIDATION VERSUS REDUCTION)

The atmosphere inside the kiln, specifically the amount of oxygen present in the kiln, will directly affect the coloration of your glazes. An oxidizing atmosphere is one in which more oxygen is present in the kiln than is needed to burn the fuel. Oxidation refers to a process of chemical recombination that occurs in a kiln that has plenty of oxygen. When heat is applied to the glaze, compounds volatilize or break apart. They then recombine with the oxygen available inside the kiln to produce a new set of oxides. Electric kilns generally oxidize, as their heat source does not require oxygen to produce heat.

In the case of reduction, a live flame, not electricity, is used to heat the kiln. The flame, whether from wood, natural gas, oil, or coal, requires oxygen to continue burning. When there is plenty of oxygen available in the kiln, you will continue to have an oxidizing atmosphere inside the kiln, no matter what fuel source you use. However, if there is not enough oxygen in the kiln for the fuel to burn completely, the result is carbon monoxide in the kiln atmosphere. The carbon atoms are naturally attracted to oxygen and will create carbon dioxide when combined with the oxygen molecules present in the clay and glaze themselves. The reduced oxygen in the clay and glaze will directly affect the coloration and texture of the finished work. For this reason, potters will intentionally reduce the amount of oxygen in the kiln by reducing air flow, hence "reduction." The difference in color can be quite radical. Look no further than a glaze with copper carbonate, which may be green in oxidizing kiln, and oxblood red in reduction.

CHAPTER 1

COMMERCIAL GLAZES VERSUS MIXING YOUR OWN

There are hundreds of commercially produced glazes that have been specifically formulated and tested by ceramic engineers to provide you with a wide-ranging palette of finishes. When applied and fired according to their instructions, these glazes are consistent, reliable, and convenient. However, their formulas are kept secret, and relative to mixing your own glazes, they can be very expensive! While mixing your own glazes can be more time-consuming than a quick trip to the store or ordering online, it is much more economical. When you purchase the materials yourself and mix your own glaze, you can save up to 80 percent versus using commercial glazes. Over the course of several kiln loads, these savings can really add up. Additionally, it is easier to adjust a recipe you mix yourself, because you know what ingredients are in the glaze.

While the cost can be an issue, quality generally is not. Glaze you mix yourself is neither superior nor inferior to commercial glazes. You should view them both as viable avenues to express yourself visually. Also, it's good to keep in mind that commercially produced glazes and glazes that you mix yourself can be used in conjunction with one another. This means you can always splurge on a unique commercial glaze and complement it with more cost-effective glazes you mix yourself.

Whether you buy commercial glaze or mix your own, it's all about getting the results you want when you unload the kiln.

PREPARING TO GLAZE

In commercial kitchens and restaurants, there is often so much prep work to be done that there is a dedicated and indispensable position, the prep cook, who comes in early to get things ready. Before a chef can prepare a dish to be served, onions must be chopped, potatoes peeled, and mushrooms cleaned of dirt. If any of these activities is overlooked or done poorly, it will affect both the taste and the presentation of the dish.

Similarly, in the glaze kitchen there are several important steps you can take to prepare a glaze that will ensure a high-quality result. This prep work makes the rest of the process flow smoothly. Be sure to pay attention to the details at this stage of the game; you will make things much easier for yourself when you begin to glaze your work.

SLAKING, MIXING, AND SIEVING

Regardless of whether you purchase commercial glaze dry or mix your own glaze from dry materials, you will need to mix it with water in three steps.

Slaking Ⓐ As a rule, you can start by filling your container one-third full of water. From here on out, make sure you are wearing a dust mask in a well-ventilated area or outdoors. Next, you'll pour the dry premixed materials for the glaze over the top of the water. Wait a minute and allow the water to work its way up through the materials. If there is not enough water to make it all the way to the top of the dry materials, you can pour more water on top until the dry materials are completely submerged. You want to err on the side of having too little water, rather than too much, as you may add more water during the next two steps.

Mixing Ⓑ Once the glaze has slaked, you can use a stir stick, whisk, or drill with a blunger attachment to mix the glaze materials thoroughly. Whichever tool you choose for mixing, move it up and down through the glaze as you mix and be thorough. Do not just stir in a circle with a stick immersed only halfway to the bottom of the bucket. Be careful with a drill and blunger, though. If you continue to spin the blunger when you pull it out of the mixture, you will glaze your legs. I've seen it many times, and I've done it more than once myself!

Sieving © Even after slaking and mixing, some coarser particles or chunks of glaze material sticking together in lumps may remain and need to be sieved. For this reason, always sieve your glaze twice after mixing it. You will need a second bucket of equal size for this. For most glazes, an 80-mesh screen is sufficient to create a smooth, flowing glaze. Glazes should be resieved before each use, as glaze can dry on the side of the bucket and fall back into the mixture, creating chunks. Also, in a community studio setting, I have found all manner of bisqueware, tools, and other foreign objects in a bucket of glaze. Screening will help you ensure that none of these end up affecting your finished product—that is, unless you were trying to make some unexpected art.

THE SPECIFICS OF SPECIFIC GRAVITY

It's a common misconception that specific gravity measures the thickness of a glaze. Specific gravity actually refers to the density of a material relative to water. Density is the measurable amount of matter per unit of volume, while thickness, for our purposes, refers to how viscous, sticky, or resistant to flow a fluid is.

As such, glaze of certain density can be made thicker by adding a flocculant (a material that promotes the clumping of particles), such as Epsom salts, or thinner by adding a deflocculant, such as Darvan 7. Gums, like CMC, will also thicken a glaze. While the addition of these materials will change the thickness of the glaze, the density will remain the same.

Measuring specific gravity is an incredibly important step in the preparation and application of glaze. The goal is to get just the right amount of glaze onto the piece, and the density of the liquid glaze will affect how much is absorbed by the bisque. Denser glaze will result in more material being absorbed by the bisque. The problem is, if the piece absorbs too much glaze, it may run right off the pot in firing. Less dense glaze will result in less material being absorbed by the bisque. Similarly, if the piece does not absorb enough glaze material, too much of the clay body will show. Both problems are avoidable by taking time to measure and adjust specific gravity to the appropriate level. Industrial ceramic facilities rely heavily on measuring specific gravity to ensure a uniform product. It used to be that few studios measured specific gravity, though I'm happy to say that is slowly changing. But the most important part is the amount of glaze that gets on the piece!

Glaze myth #278: Dipping your finger in a bucket of glaze to see if it runs off your fingernail is a great way to measure glaze density.

Assuredly, somewhere in your travels, someone in a clay studio has delighted in showing you the "finger dip" method of measuring glaze density. This wise potter will mix (and usually forget to screen) a bucket of glaze, then will

---

A hydrometer is a worthwhile investment to measure the density of your glazes.

dip his bare finger into some perhaps question-ably soluble or toxic materials, hold his finger aloft proudly, and beam at you as he says, "See? It's running off my fingernail. Just right!" Alternatively, he may have compared the glaze to a dairy product. For example, he'll say, "That glaze looks a little dense, like cream. It should be more like skim milk. Why don't you add a little water?" He'll make deep eye contact and nod knowingly.

These methods of analyzing specific gravity are rooted in good intentions. While they do, in fact, indicate relative degrees of a glaze's den-sity—and can even get good results with some glazes—more accurate tools exist to measure the specific gravity of your glaze. I would sug-gest that you rely on measuring specific gravity using a hydrometer, or by measuring the weight of 1,000 milliliters of glaze.

The hydrometer is designed to sink into a liquid until it is buoyed. It will sink deeper into a less dense glaze than into a denser glaze. The specific gravity of the glaze relative to water is calibrated on the outside of the hydrome-ter. Take the reading at the level of the glaze. The specific gravity of water is theoretically 1.00 g/ml, although this measurement would have to be taken at sea level with a room temperature of 70 degrees Fahrenheit. (With substantial elevation or a different tempera-ture, that calibration will change slightly. For our purposes, though, it serves as a good base measurement.) All glazes will have SG mea-surements higher than that of water. The higher the SG number, the denser the glaze. Most glazes work well at SG 1.45, although proper testing should be done, as some glazes, such as Anja's Silky Clear (page 164), and Odys-sey Clear (page 173), which look milky when thickly applied, benefit from lower specific gravities. This is due to the unique gelling property of Gerstley Borate, resulting in a more viscous consistency. I recommend applying those two at SG 1.25 and 1.35, respectively. Alternatively, other glazes look best when applied more thickly, such as Chun Celadon (page 171), which looks best at SG 1.55.

Another method used to measure specific gravity is to weigh 1,000 milliliters of glaze with a scale. This works because 1 milliliter of water weighs 1 gram (at room temperature at sea level). Therefore, 1,000 milliliters of water (theoretically) weighs 1,000 grams. Again, as the molecules in the glaze are "denser" than water, 1,000 milliliters of glaze will weigh more than 1,000 grams. Try both methods to see which one you like best. Once you choose the method you prefer, stick to it for consistency. Note that you may measure 100, 10, or even 1 gram of glaze and it will give you an assess-ment of the specific gravity, although the decimal place will be moved. If you measure 1,000 milliliters of glaze and it weighs 1,450 grams, measuring 100 milliliters of the same glaze will weigh 145 grams, 10 milliliters of the same glaze will weigh 14.5 grams, and 1 millili-ter of glaze will weigh 1.45 grams. These are all acceptable methods that indicate the density relative to water.

Keep in mind that once you have established the specific gravity of a glaze, the second factor that determines how much glaze ends up on your pot is the length of time the pot comes in contact with the glaze and the absorption rate of bisque whether through dipping, pouring, or spraying. We'll get into glaze application start-ing on page 38.

CHANGING CONSISTENCY

A couple of things can happen if your glaze's specific gravity is not within the appropriate range (1.45 for most glazes listed in this book unless otherwise indicated). A glaze that has low specific gravity won't give you a thick enough coat. A glaze that is too dense will likely go on too thickly and may crack off, or worse, run off the side of your pot during the firing. Before glazing, sieve your glaze into a clean bucket and measure the specific gravity. If it is

If your glaze is too thin and it separates out with a layer of water after settling overnight, you can remove some water with a measuring cup and then remix the glaze.

PREPPING WORK TO BE GLAZED

Just as the glaze needs to be prepared, your bisque fired work needs to be prepped before glazing. First, check the work for any sharp edges or burs and sand them down. It is much easier to do this now than when the clay has vitrified further. Next, remove all dust from the pot. Some people dip their pots in water, but this will saturate the bisque, and so it will absorb less glaze. Potters who do this must wait overnight for their work to dry or adjust their glaze recipes accordingly, using a higher specific gravity. Others sponge the surface with a damp sponge, but this too introduces some water and takes practice to get right. The way I prefer to prepare work is to blow it off with an air gun, with the air compressor set to 60 to 80 psi.

Note: Always wear a dust mask or respirator when sanding or cleaning bisque with a spray gun. Use a spray booth or do it outdoors to avoid raising a cloud of ceramic dust in the studio.

within range, you can begin glazing, knowing that the glaze is at just the right density. If it is too dense, you can add water a little bit at time, resieve, and remeasure the specific gravity until it is just right. If the glaze is not dense enough, you must let some of the water evaporate out, which may take some time. In order to do so, leave your bucket uncovered overnight. Then you'll mix the glaze, sieve, and measure the specific gravity again. If you have thickened it excessively by evaporating too much water, you can add water back and resieve until you get it right. This may seem like a lot of work, but really you are trading time spent before glazing for time totally wasted if your pots don't turn out right. If you are assiduous in this practice, you will save many pots from bad glazing—and thus save yourself from many headaches.

TESTING

For best results, always test new glazes as soon as you get them or mix them, but before using them to glaze in earnest. You may want to experiment with different specific gravities or over different-colored clays or slips. When you're testing, I recommend using what I call "meaningful" test tiles. Most studios have a test tile board made from objects that have little aesthetic value. These may be simple extruded cylinders or the classic upside-down T shapes that can be made on the wheel by throwing a low, wide, bottomless cylinder with exaggerated feet both inside and out. Using a wire, you cut under the cylinder. The wire can then be used to cut the cylinder into sixteen to twenty-four test tiles.

Meaningful test tiles should be similar to the work you create, even if your work is sculptural, as in these press-molded busts by Kathleen Lizzul.

A meaningful test tile is one that accurately represents the kind of work you want to make. If you use slips, make sure your test tile has slips on it. If you use lots of texture, make sure your test tile reflects that. The classic upside-down T-shaped tile is one of the quickest forms to make. It can be useful in scenarios such as doing line blends, described below, or testing when you don't have much time to spare.

But what if your test "tiles" could be more than tiles? If a test turns out well, and it's on a cup form (as the tiles are on page 33), the test piece could be its own art object to be treasured, gifted, or even sold. I have sold many of my test pieces over the years, and as a professional potter, it is a way that I can pay myself for the time I spent testing. If you want to do this, I recommend that you find a form that accurately represents your work—

one that you could make out of wet clay in approximately 3 minutes. If you spend 1 hour per month making meaningful test tiles, you will have twenty pieces available for your testing. That's 240 tests per year. If you make sure to put at least several test pieces in every firing, you will soon discover great new glazes and combinations, and you'll be well on your way to amazing glaze!

A SIMPLE APPROACH TO LINE BLENDS

Another key strategy in testing is to methodically discover the possibilities of combining glazes. What follows is a simple approach called the line blend that can be used with glazes you already have available and that will result in dozens of new possibilities.

A line blend can be as simple as combining two glazes 50/50. This line blend shows 100 percent Oxblood, 50/50 Oxblood and Reitz Green, and 100 percent Reitz green, from left to right.

Simply put, a line blend takes two ingredients and blends them in different proportions at regular intervals. The simplest line blend would be to mix two glazes in the following percentages: 100/0, 50/50, and 0/100. In this way, you can see unadulterated glazes as well as glazes mixed together. You can make the intervals smaller to see more variations: 100/0, 75/25, 50/50, 25/75, and 0/100. Decreasing the interval to 10 percent will yield even more variations: 100/0, 90/10, 80/20, 70/30, 60/40, 50/50, 40/60, 30/70, 20/80, 10/90, and 0/100. This may be done either with dry materials (by weighing them out) or with wet glaze measure by volume. With the wet glaze method, be sure also to weigh out the amount of water used in the mix so you can replicate it in future mixes. Make sure you label your test tiles!

Note: Triaxial and quadraxial blends utilize the same principal as the line blend but use three and four ingredients, respectively. Rather than a line of possible blends, these methods of testing result in a triangular or square grid of possibilities.

A simple triaxial blend will look like this:

Ingredient A
Ingredient B
Ingredient C

```
                    AAAAA
               AAAAB      AAAAC
          AAABB      AAABC      AAACC
     AABBB      AABBC      AABCC      AACCC
ABBBB      ABBBC      ABBCC      ABCCC      ACCCC
BBBBB  BBBBC  BBBCC  BBCCC  BCCCC  CCCCC
```

GALLERY

A word on the galleries in this book: I wanted to share a collection of pieces that are sure to inspire. To that end, this first gallery is full of work to excite you about the possibilities of glaze. For the galleries that follow, the artists' work will relate to the concepts shared in the preceding chapter. Note that the galleries feature many glazes that potters have developed through years of hard work, as well as commercial glazes. (The recipes in Chapter 6 are not intended to match the galleries, which is why they have their own test tiles.) I encourage you to explore these pieces with an open mind and let these top artists inspire further discovery!

Blue Vase Detail.
John Britt.
Photo courtesy of the artist.

Sometimes a single glaze can provide a wonderfully variegated surface, as in this detail shot of a narrow-necked bottle by John Britt.

Pair of Steins. Steven Hill. *Photo courtesy of the artist.*

These inviting steins have been layered with several complimentary glazes. The microcrystals at the rim are subtle, but they add an additional layer of depth.

Covered Jar. Nich Daunis. *Photo courtesy of Halima Flynt.*

A single coat of beautiful glaze will accentuate strong form. See Chapter 2 for more on single coat glazes.

Oil Spot Pill Jar. Frank Vickery. *Photo courtesy of the artist.*

The green-glazed lid of Frank Vickery's jar showcases his decorative slipwork, while the oil-spot glaze on the side of the piece provides a second area of visual interest.

Thicket Jar. Ben Carter. *Photo courtesy of the artist.*

The unglazed form can be thought of as a canvas for painterly techniques, as in this covered jar by Ben Carter. Brushwork will be covered in Chapter 2.

GALLERY

Cloudscape Emergence. Sam Chung. *Photo courtesy of the artist.*

Black and red highlights against a background of white glaze provide a potent color contrast in the unmistakable work of Sam Chung. Developing a personal aesthetic will be discussed in the next chapter.

Pocket Vase with Figures. Nick Joerling. *Photo courtesy of the artist.*

Two contrasting glazes accentuate each other. The imagery is created through the use of wax resists, which will be described in Chapter 3.

Camper Plate. Laurie Caffery Harris.
Photo courtesy of the artist.

Inlaid washes and watercolor underglaze decoration look best under a bright clear glaze in this whimsical platter. See Chapter 3 for more information on underglazes.

Ms. Rosetta and Friends. Taylor Robenalt.
Photo courtesy of the artist.

This lively bird duo features many of the techniques that will be described in this book, including underglazes, glazes, and lusters. Taylor Robenalt's use of porcelain provides a bright white background that allows the colors to really pop.

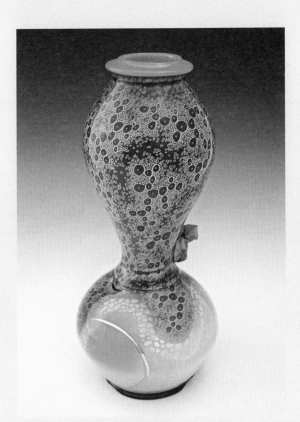

Vessel. Adrian Sandstrom. *Photo courtesy of the artist.*

This dynamic surface was built up using every trick in the book. The narrow, bulbous form is accentuated by the use of slips, underglazes, glazes, and lusters, all of which will be covered in the coming chapters.

Tiny Bowls. Deborah Schwartzkopf.
Photo courtesy of the artist.

These tiny bowls are an excellent example of the type of piece that can be quickly produced to serve as a great canvas for glaze tests.

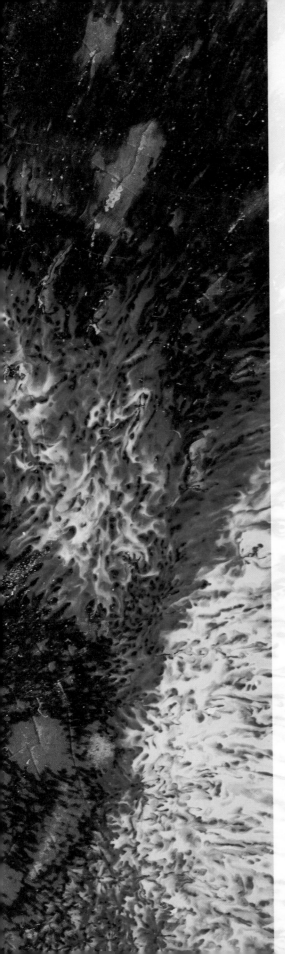

2

APPLYING GLAZE (AKA THE DANCE)

Glaze myth #215: *Glazing isn't fun.*

You may have encountered people who badmouth glazing. You may have even met people who *hate* glazing. You know the type: they would rather do just about anything (even clean the studio!) other than glaze their work. These people often see glazing as a necessary step to finishing a piece. They must check it off the to-do list to get back to the more enjoyable process of working with wet clay.

It is true that glazing can be intimidating, especially when you have fear of ruining a good pot with bad—or perhaps worse, boring—glaze. If you or your studio mates are in the "hate it" camp, chances are there's more you can fix than the recipes you use. What you need is a good, old-fashioned reframing of the way you look at glazing a piece! Rather than drudgery, try thinking of glaze application as a form of dance. With this reframing, you can infuse the process with a sense of joy and wonder, while simultaneously exploring the endless possibilities that glaze offers to enhance your work. Before you can go on *Dancing with the Stars*, however, you first must learn the dance steps. In this chapter, we'll look at the primary methods of applying glaze and how to proceed with grace, agility, and confidence.

While most ceramic artists enjoy the tactile bliss of wet clay running through their hands on the potter's wheel or the satisfaction of carving a beautiful line on leather-hard clay, the glazing process offers its own satisfying movements and moments, which we will explore in depth in this chapter. Feel free to crank up the tunes to choreograph your movements (use headphones in a community setting), and let's boogie.

GLAZE DESIGN: FORMING A PLAN

Wait a minute! Before the music starts, we should do a little planning. It is extremely important to go into glazing with a goal and to take a systematic approach. Haphazard glazing will result in haphazard results. Just as you may have spent time sketching or looking in books for inspiration to create your forms out of wet clay, you should spend an equal amount of time sketching glaze combinations in color and researching other artists whose glazes inspire you. I recommend that you make an inspiration board for yourself. Keep it in your studio and update it often.

SET YOUR INTENTION

Examine what it is you like about each of the pieces on your inspiration board and make notes. Seek to expand upon your inspirations in ways that are meaningful to you. An important question to ask yourself is "What do I have to say?" Each choice you make aesthetically results in a visual statement. These choices you make along the way, including the colors you choose to work with, carry with them your unique way of looking at the world. This will, of course, influence those who view your pieces. The painter Wassily Kandinsky makes this clear in his book *Concerning the Spiritual in Art*, providing an excellent overview of the use of color and its psychological impact on the viewer. For example, according to Kandinsky, the fiery red of oxblood glazes and the icy blue of some celadons will stimulate the observer differently, alternatively warming or cooling the viewer's psyche depending on which color is used.

Sketching with the medium of your choice is a great way to hone in on a glazing plan.

SKETCHING IN COLOR

This is an extremely important exercise when you are interested in developing as a glaze artist, and it will help separate you from the crowd. Buy a set of good-quality markers, colored pencils, or oil pastels—whatever medium you like best. Personally, I like to use a fine-point Sharpie to sketch the outline of a piece, and thicker markers to fill in the color. I usually sketch the pot freehand, but you can use a piece of graph paper if you are interested in really nailing the form. You can then photocopy the blank form and color it in different ways. Try out a variety of different color schemes to see which one suits you the best. If you are technologically inclined, you can use computer-aided design (CAD) software to design your pieces, add color, and get a glimpse of what the piece will look like in 3D. Your sketches should function to work out your ideas; they do not have to be masterpieces. What is important is that *you* understand what you mean by the marks

When your forms and your glaze work together to create a personal aesthetic, it's a beautiful thing. Look no further than this set by Sara Ballek.

you have made. Fashion designers often work in this manner, sketching in their own style to create a dramatic impression of the effect they want to achieve. You will work out the technicalities later.

These preparatory exercises will pay serious dividends when you begin glazing. No more wondering, "How should I glaze this piece?" as you stare at your studio's test tiles, hoping that your eye can come up with a satisfying combination on the fly. With a plan in mind and your intention set, and having sketched colorful glaze designs that line up with your personal aesthetic, you should move one solid step away from "I hate glazing."

DEVELOPING A PERSONAL AESTHETIC

Developing a personal aesthetic may seem like a lofty goal. However, on a daily basis, you make numerous decisions that reflect what you value artistically and how you view the world. For inspiration, look to your own fashion sense and the way you decorate your living space. Are there commonalities there? What colors make you feel most at home, at peace? What colors energize you? What textures and patterns are you most attracted to? You know that you are on the right path when your mug matches your shirt.

Search other areas of your life for meaningful pattern, designs, and imagery. Look at childhood photos, your favorite band's poster art, that secret spot where you like to watch the sunset. This is a sure approach toward an authentic glazing style that represents your values. In the end, we can always return to that profoundly simple but important question: "What do I have to say?" Your glazing should reflect the answer to this question and be a means to articulate your individuality.

Cayce Kolstad and the Happy Accident

Cayce Kolstad can move mountains. I've seen him do it. I once watched him dig up a 600-pound rock from his yard and move it by himself to create a stair from his wood-fired pizza oven to his back yard archery range. A larger-than-life character from Lexington, Kentucky, Cayce is also a gentle spirit with a devoted following of young potters who have taken his kids' classes at Odyssey over the years.

Known for his Cayceroles, beautiful stoneware casseroles that sell out every time he makes a run of them, and for several innovative thrown and altered chip-and-dip forms, Cayce also loves firing the gas kiln at Odyssey. The medieval-meets-1970s folk look of his ceramics has a timeless appeal.

One firing at Odyssey left us mystified when the bucket that had been labeled Reitz Green (see recipe page 166), normally a variegated black and green glaze in cone 10, had turned out as a beautiful lavender. At first we thought it may have been an anomaly in the firing, but subsequent firings with the same batch of glaze yielded the same results. We put it on everything until the bucket ran out, but nobody could figure out how the purple had been achieved. Detective Cayce was on it. Theorizing that it was possible that someone had mistaken Oxblood (recipe page 163) for Reitz Green, both of which are a light sage color in their wet, unfired stage, Cayce did a line blend (see page 33) of the two glazes together and found that between 70/30 and 30/70, the combination of the two glazes resulted in varying shades of purple. The resulting glaze, Purple Passion Plum (page 169) is now a mainstay at Odyssey.

Covered Jar. Cayce Kolstad. *Photo courtesy of the artist.*

Purple Passion Plum (page 169) was developed by Cayce Kolstad by running a line blend of Oxblood and Reitz Green (pages 163 and 166).

Handled Basket. Cayce Kolstad. *Photo courtesy of the artist.*

A single coat of high-gloss glaze breaks in the grooves of this thrown and altered basket.

Casserole and Covered Jar. Cayce Kolstad. *Photo by Tim Robison.*

Another of Cayce's famous Caycerole dishes and a lidded jar.

Casserole. Cayce Kolstad. *Photo courtesy of the artist.*

The interior of this casserole is lined with Buttermilk (page 160), a durable, food-safe glaze. The interior of casseroles showcase food best when a lighter color is used.

BASIC APPLICATION
(AKA GLAZE KITCHEN CHOREOGRAPHY)

Okay, now that you've warmed up, so to speak, it is time to work on your moves! You can think of the glaze and your bisque as your dance partners, and you are the lead. First, make sure that you have all your tools and cleanup materials ready to go. You will need a bucket of water and a large sponge to clean up drips or spills, tongs or gloves for dipping, pitchers for pouring, squeeze bottles for trailing, and a good respirator or dust mask if you are going to be using the spray booth. You may want to stretch a bit to warm up, as glazing uses your whole body.

Applying glaze is, of course, the central focus of this book: the goal is to get just the right amount of glaze exactly where you want it. Too much, and you will be grinding glaze off of your kiln shelves; too little, and the clay body will show through. Both missteps create thoroughly undesirable results. But by using the techniques that follow, you will gain control over the materials you are using, and you'll be able to achieve the results you want with confidence and regularity.

Although it may take a couple of tries to figure out some of the moves, soon you will master the *tenmoku* two-step, the Shino shuffle, and the ash glaze arabesque. Have fun, keep it light, and "dance like nobody is watching!"

A QUICK WORD ON SPECIFIC GRAVITY AND DEPTH GAUGES

There are several important factors at play in getting just the right amount of glaze onto your piece. The first is the density relative to water, or specific gravity, of the glaze that you are using. The specific gravity of the glaze is of crucial importance to the glazing process. You want to take the time to measure specific gravity of the glaze each time you start, as water can evaporate out of a bucket and change the density overnight. Note that there is not a universal specific gravity that works best for all glazes. Some will perform better when dense; other glazes require less density. Likewise, you'll want to adjust the gravity based on your application method. (Spraying, for example, requires a less dense glaze due to the equipment used, whereas glazes that are brushed on benefit from higher density.) Only through testing will you be able to establish the ideal specific gravity for each of your glazes. (For more on specific gravity, see page 28.)

Once a piece is glazed, you can measure the amount of glaze that has built up on the surface of your pot using a depth gauge. A depth gauge is a measuring device with a fine needle on its end that you can press through the glaze to the surface of your pot. When the bar of the depth gauge meets the surface of the glaze, the gauge will measure the thickness of the glaze. Depth gauges range in price, and if cost is a factor, you may use a needle tool and ruler to achieve the same measurement. To do this, press the needle through the glaze and use your thumbnail to mark the place on the needle where the glaze ends. You can then measure the distance from the end of your thumbnail to the end of the needle against a ruler to determine the thickness of the glaze. There's a range of thickness (1 to 4 millimeters) that may be ideal, depending on the glaze you are using.

It is important to note that glazes will perform better or worse depending on their thickness, and each glaze will need to have its ideal thickness established before you begin glazing in earnest. As always, testing and detailed note taking will benefit you enormously. For your tests, be sure to write down the specific gravity of the glaze, the application details, and the thickness of the glaze on your piece. After

A depth gauge in action.

your pieces have been fired, take further notes. If the glaze is too thin, you can either increase the specific gravity or apply more glaze. (For example, maybe you'll submerge the piece for a longer period of time when dipping or apply an extra coat when spraying.) Conversely, if the glaze is too thick, you can decrease the specific gravity or reduce the amount of glaze you apply (by again altering variables, such as submerging the piece for a shorter period of time or spraying one less coat of glaze). Retest until you get it just right. It may take work to get there, but when you do, you'll have perfectly repeatable results!

DIPPING

Dipping your piece is the fastest way to cover part or all of your piece in a smooth coat of glaze. You will want to use an appropriate glaze container for the shape of the piece you are glazing. Taller, more vertical forms can often be dipped directly into the glaze bucket using a pair of tongs or gloved hands. Wider, more horizontal forms, such as shallow bowls, plates, and platters, are best dipped in a lower, wider container such as a pebble bowl or bus tub. The goal with dipping is to create the smoothest coat of glaze possible. Glazes may move on their own when melting, but unintentional drips from careless glazing are almost always unattractive. To ensure uniformity, and to avoid that unattractive drip, you can use several techniques that aid in creating a smooth coat of glaze.

Note: When dipping forms, most potters use wax to coat the bottoms of their pieces before dipping. This keeps glaze from sticking to the foot of the pot, which can then cause it to fuse to the kiln shelf. Cleanup is as easy as one pass with a moist sponge to remove any stubborn glaze. For a detailed description of wax and wax resist techniques, see page 77.

THE COUNT

Using this technique, you will be factoring the specific gravity of the glaze in conjunction with the amount of time the piece is submerged to create an individualized approach to glazing your work. Both factors in the equation, the specific gravity and the length of time submerged, will affect the amount of glaze that ends up on your piece. In other words, a denser glaze will take less time submerged in glaze to build up to the ideal thickness than a less dense glaze will. Our goal is to establish the ideal thickness of glaze on the piece, and to use specific gravity and a count method to be able to replicate it.

Several tools are helpful in measuring specific gravity and in determining the thickness of the glaze on your piece. See page 28 for a refresher on specific gravity.

Once you have established the specific gravity of the glaze, you can glaze your test tiles. It is important to submerge the tiles in glaze for equal amounts of time. At Odyssey, we recommend submerging the tile for 2 seconds as a starting point. You can count "one, one thousand, two, one thousand" in your head, but we have found that this is a highly subjective affair, depending upon the speed at which you articulate your thoughts, as well as on the amount of coffee you consumed prior to coming to the studio. Use a clock or timer instead.

Here's how to dip a vertical form:

1. Make sure that the glaze bucket sits at a good height, so you don't have to bend over excessively. Waist level works best.

2. Using tongs or gloved hands for larger work, submerge your piece in the well-mixed, screened glaze with the appropriate specific gravity. As you are lowering the piece into the glaze, angle it slightly so the glaze flows smoothly into the interior of the piece, rather than splashing as it rushes in over the lip.

3. Completely submerge the piece in glaze for a 2-second count, then remove the piece and invert it over the bucket to pour out any glaze on the inside. This will also help keep the coat uniform, as the bottom of the piece has spent slightly more time submerged than the top has. Inverting the piece causes the thicker glaze at the bottom of the piece to spread out evenly toward the top.

4. Hold the piece over the bucket until it has stopped dripping, then place it right-side up on the table to dry.

When you dip pieces upside down, an air bubble forms to keep the glaze from moving to the interior of the piece. This can be especially useful when dipping an accent glaze over a base glaze.

Here's how to dip a horizontal form:

1. For horizontal forms, you may want to use a bus tub or pebble bowl and channel lock tongs. Channel lock tongs hold the piece from the side, allowing you to dip horizontally through the glaze without straining your wrist.

2. It is important to use a "first-side-in-first side-out" strategy to ensure that all parts of the piece spend an equal amount of time submerged.

3. Once the entire piece is submerged, use a 2-second count, smoothly remove the piece from the glaze, and invert it over the container to allow any drips to run off.

4. Once all the drips are gone, set the piece right-side up on the table and allow to dry before touching.

You may choose to dip only a portion of the piece in glaze, either right-side up or upside down, depending on where you want the coat. For a single coat applied to only a portion of your piece, the same best practices apply. You should be moving smoothly and with intention, altering the dip angle or using a wax resist to apply the glaze exactly where you want it. In general, layered glazes should be kept toward the top of the piece in the case of glazes that tend to run. However, there are some combinations of glazes that do not move, in which case you can glaze all the way to the bottom of the piece. While a more thorough discussion of layering can be found on page 55, the key to most combinations is getting just the right amount of the second (or third) coat of glaze exactly where you want it—just like the first coat.

Again, using a wax resist (page 77) is a sure-fire way to protect portions of the piece from receiving glaze. When you're inverting a piece to dip it, you'll often want to create an air bubble on the inside of the piece—keeping the second, layered coat of glaze on the exterior only. When you're doing this, you want to avoid the "bloop." The bloop is caused by the air trapped inside the piece when inverted. It occurs when you angle the piece on the way out, allowing that trapped air to escape out one side or the other, often causing an unwanted splash of glaze on the outside or inside of your piece, accompanied by the namesake *bloop!* sound. To avoid the bloop, carefully remove the piece from the glaze, making sure to keep it level, with the lip and foot of the piece parallel to the floor. If time allows, you can wax the inside of the piece, which will also alleviate this problem.

With practice, pouring should create as even of a coat of glaze as dipping.

POURING

Pouring glaze allows you to glaze only a certain area of a piece—the inside rim of a platter, for example. You can also use pouring to glaze work too large to fit in a bucket, as we'll see in the next chapter, in the section on glazing large pieces. Pouring glaze can be a quite satisfying and beautiful process. As liquid glaze cascades out of the pitcher and is quickly absorbed on the surface of your pieces, you can see fluid dynamics at work. As anyone who has seen the slow motion of a drop of milk can attest, there is a certain beauty to fluid in motion. It can create its own unique decorative pattern.

To ensure success when pouring, find a pitcher that pours cleanly, without drips. You will also need to hold the piece over a bucket or other container to recapture any glaze that runs off the piece and to avoid a messy cleanup. When you're pouring a glaze, it is more difficult to work with a count system, so I'd recommend abandoning that strategy and applying two coats of poured glaze, or enough to roughly equal one 2-second dip.

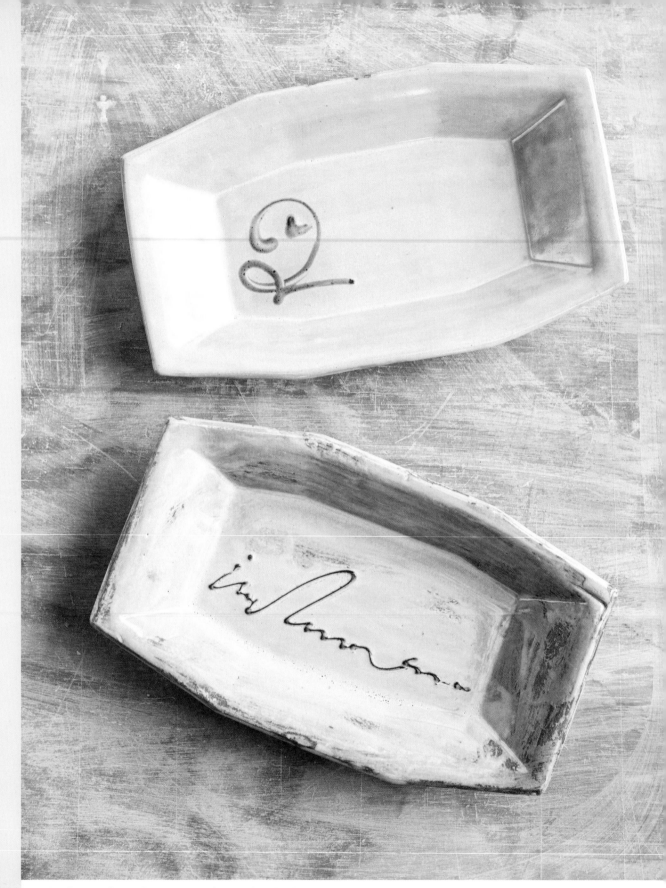

Brushing can be used to create a uniform surface (top) or one with variation (bottom).

BRUSHING

Brushing glaze onto a piece can be an incredibly satisfying endeavor. If you love the feel of a brush in your hands, this method of application will appeal to you. Most glaze recipes require additives in order for the glaze to flow smoothly off your brush. You may want to add a bit of gum arabic, glycerin, liquid starch, or commercial products such as Veegum T or CMC gum to your glaze to increase its brushability. (Pay attention to the instructions accompanying these materials, as each requires a different amount to be added to the glaze.) While this may slow the drying time, your brushwork will be made much easier. The challenge when brushing glaze is to create an even coat, which must be done multiple times. It usually takes about three coats of brushed glaze to equal one 2-second dip.

Here are a few tips:

- Alternate the directions of the brushstrokes to ensure that the strokes fill one another and create a uniform coat.

- Allow the glaze to dry between coats.

- Choose a soft-bristled brush that can be charged with a fair amount of glaze. Hard-bristled brushes leave deep grooves and make it difficult to get an even coat of glaze. (Potter Joe Campbell has a wonderful side business making brushes specifically for use with glaze. If you get a chance to own one of Joe's brushes, jump at the opportunity. They are themselves small works of art and a joy to use.)

You can also use brushing in a more decorative fashion. You can brush glaze directly onto the surface of the pot, creating patterns or images, or onto a base layer of glaze. When painted over another layer of glaze, this procedure is referred to as in-glaze painting.

Note how the trailed red line of underglaze on the pre-fired work (right) translates to a dynamic red point of interest when fired (left). Glazes used are Spearmint (page 178) and Chun Celadon (page 171).

TRAILING

Glaze trailing is another effective means of applying glaze. It provides effects unattainable by other methods. Glaze trailers (essentially any kind of squeeze bottle) come in myriad sizes; start by choosing one that most closely matches the line you want to create. You can trail glazes above or below other coats of glaze. Glazing in this manner allows you to work with imagery, either concrete or abstract, and also allows you to create fine lines with your glaze.

You can make some very dynamic colors by combining commercial underglazes with clear or translucent glazes. For example, I use Amaco's Radiant Red underglaze mixed 50/50 with Chun Celadon to create a bright red at cone 6. The underglaze by itself is very matte, and the addition of the Chun helps it meld with the other glazes. The result is a bright red line that adds dynamism to the glaze combination.

SPRAYING

The spray booth may conjure up images of the Jersey shore and its colorful airbrushed T-shirts. I have always been amazed by the artists who create those shirts, custom designed on the spot, with just a few quick, efficient sweeps of the arm. Spraying glaze is a similar process, though the results are generally far from an airbrushed shirt!

The main advantage to spraying is that it allows you to feather your glazes, creating a gradient effect on the piece. It is very difficult to achieve this effect any other way. Spraying glaze has other benefits, as well. With the spray gun, you can introduce a very thin coat of glaze to a piece, or you can build up a thicker coat of glaze in certain areas. Spraying glaze can also be an effective way to glaze large pieces that will not fit in any container.

You will notice that when you're spraying, the glaze lands on the pots differently than when you're dipping or brushing. Glaze builds up on the surface in a powdery topography rather than being drawn into the porous surface of the bisque. However, if you continue to spray in the same area, it will eventually develop a sheen. Once the glaze looks wet, you can move to a different section of the piece. Cover the entire area desired, and once it has dried, return for one more wet coat. The amount of glaze that accumulates on your piece will be the rough equivalent of one 2-second dip.

Here are a few important tips for spraying glaze:

- Always wear a respirator or dust mask to avoid inhaling aerated glaze.

- Always spray your glazes in a well-ventilated spray booth or outdoors.

- Most people use 35 to 45 psi when spraying.

- Always sieve your glaze with an 80-mesh sieve to avoid clogging up the nozzle of the gun.

- For a denser glaze, you may want to lower the specific gravity with a little water to improve its sprayability.

- HVLP guns have a nozzle that allows you to adjust the shape of spray coming out of the gun. Rather than just a circular spray that comes out of a standard spray gun, HVLP guns can also emit a vertical or horizontal oval-shaped spray. These different spray shapes can give your sprayed work a different look, and are good for feathering layered glazes.

- Be careful when you handle work that has been sprayed with glaze, unless you want to leave your fingerprints in the powdery surface, only to show up later, when you unload the kiln!

Don't be intimated by the spray booth in your studio. It is the best way to experiment with thinner coats of glaze and feathering effects.

SINGLE COAT

Applying a single coat of glaze may seem like the bare minimum you can do when glazing a pot. However, with just a single glaze, there are many possibilities. When combined with an interesting surface (see page 69, left), sometimes a single coat is all that's needed. Likewise, you may find glazes that are exceptional on their own.

Want to try a showstopping single-coat glaze? These five glazes look so good that they have become legendary among clay artists. Each provides a beautiful color, texture, and feel to ceramic work. The five glazes can certainly be used in conjunction with other glazes as well. (Recipes are listed starting on page 158.)

Yellow Salt (cone 10): A bucket of Yellow Salt can be found in almost every community studio, and with good reason. Yellow Salt looks great in reduction, salt, and wood kilns. It can fire as a warm yellow mottled with brown spots and will sometimes go white in a wood kiln. It is not too glossy and doesn't run. About 2 to 4 millimeters of glaze works best. See the photo on page 168.

Tenmoku (cone 10): Classic Tenmoku provides a deep glossy black when applied thickly, and it breaks beautifully on texture and edges, revealing a warm brown. The combination of colors is serious, even somber, but also calming and quieting. Perhaps for this reason, it is often associated with the practice of drinking tea. Getting just the right thickness of Tenmoku on your piece is crucial to achieving both the brown and black tones: 2 millimeters is recommended. Edges may be scraped back with a metal rib to accentuate the black/brown contrast. See the photo on page 166.

Charcoal Satin (cone 6): Charcoal Satin is another glaze with a serious feel. It looks like a well-tailored wool suit and works nicely in any environment where the other neutral colors (black, white, and gray) are present. It will break darker black where thicker and gray where thinner, providing two complementary tones in the same glaze. Charcoal Satin looks best when applied on the thick side: approximately 3 millimeters. See the photo on page 175.

Spearmint (cone 6): Originally published in Ron Roy and John Hesselberth's book *Mastering Cone 6 Glazes*, Spearmint is a lovely, mottled sage green. It is one of the most popular glazes at Odyssey because of its consistency and variegated surface. Spearmint looks great on its own, but it also "plays well with others" and can be used in many combinations. See page 57 for a stunning, layered glaze combination that uses Spearmint as a base. About 2 to 3 millimeters thick works best for Spearmint. See the photo on page 178.

Sparkle (cone 05): As its name suggests, Sparkle is a brilliant low-fire glaze that glints in the sunlight. It features a warm brown base with gold highlights. A thicker application (3 millimeters) usually works better for Sparkle. See the photo on page 184.

LAYERING GLAZES

While there's nothing wrong with single coat, you may find that you are looking for different effects that can come only from using multiple glazes on the same piece. Layering glazes can take an infinite number of forms, and can employ any or all of the application methods mentioned earlier in the chapter. Some glazes that look terrible on their own make great modifiers when layered with other glazes. Strontium Crystal Magic at cone 6 and The Juice at cone 10 are good examples. Alone, these high-titanium glazes are both a matte yellowish white. However, when layered with other glazes, they can add variations and white crystals that look like snowfall or a cascading rainbow waterfall. (See the examples on pages 57, 58, 60, and 61.)

While many artists closely guard their glaze recipes and combinations, I have always shared my secrets with my students. When they try these combinations, it piques their interest in creating combinations that better represent their own personal aesthetic. Soon enough, they have come up with combinations and variations that dance to their own music. In that spirit, I want to present twelve tried-and-true layering combinations. Test them out, but be aware that they will look different on different clay bodies. Then modify them to your taste and make them your own. This is part of the adventure in glazing: first tracing the steps of those who have come before you, then setting out on your own.

Before we dive in, here are some general guidelines for layering:

- Glazes in combination can form what is called a "eutectic," which is two or more materials that, when combined, have a lower melting point than any of them individually. For our purposes, that means glazes that do not run very much individually might run down the side of the pot when combined. For this reason, always use cookies when firing glazed work. (Cookies are fired disks of kiln-washed clay that your piece can sit on. For an in-depth description of cookies, see page 138.) Until you get to know the combination well, keep the second layer of glaze no more than one-third of the way down from the top of the pot. For tiered layering—that is, combinations that involve a third or even fourth glaze—keep these one-fourth of the way down the pot, or at the very lip, at least to start.

- Layering multiple glazes will build up increasing amounts of glaze on your pot. If the glaze is too thick, it will eventually begin to crack and fall off the work. Use a lower specific gravity on the second and third layers, submerge the piece in glaze for a shorter period of time, or use brushing or spraying to apply thinner coats.

- Always let glazes dry between coats. In some cases, you may need to use a fan to dry the work, or leave it out overnight. Make sure you give the last coat of glaze time to dry before loading pieces into the kiln as well.

12 TRIED-AND-TRUE LAYERING COMBINATIONS

CONE 6 COMBINATIONS

OASIS

1. Dip entire pot in Odyssey White Gloss.

2. Dip top third in Chun Celadon.

3. Dip Strontium Crystal Magic at rim.

BLACK-TIE AFFAIR

1. Dip entire pot in Odyssey White Gloss.

2. Dip one third of pot in Chun Celadon.

3. Dip entire pot in Charcoal Satin.

FIRELAKE

1. Dip entire pot in Fat Cat Red.

2. Dip to one-third of pot in Chun Celadon.

3. Dip rim of pot in Spearmint or Ol' Blue.

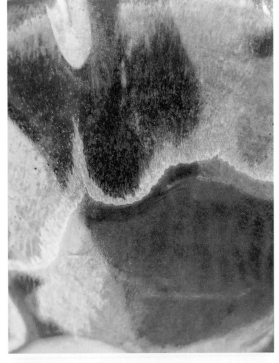

PISGAH FOREST *(Also shown on page 20)*

1. Dip whole piece in Spearmint.

2. Dip top one-third of the pot in Chun Celadon.

3. Apply red trailer line one-fourth of the way down from the top of the piece.

4. Dip Strontium Crystal Magic at rim.

MIDNIGHT IN MAINE

1. Dip whole pot in Ol' Blue.

2. Dip top one-third in Chun Celadon.

3. Apply red trailer line one-fourth of the way down from the top of the piece.

4. Dip Strontium Crystal Magic at rim.

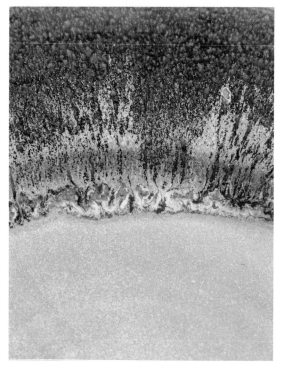

SNORKELING IN SAINT JOHN

1. Dip whole piece in Chun Celadon.

2. Dip top one-third of the piece in Strontium Crystal Magic.

3. Apply red trailer line one-fourth of the way down from the top of the piece.

4. Dip Ol' Blue at rim.

FOREST MEETS THE BEACH

(Also shown on pages 130 and 141)

1. Dip entire pot in Roger's Green.

2. Spray Yellow Salt over the entire exterior surface.

DESERT SUNRISE *(Also shown on page 43)*

1. Dip entire piece in Purple Passion Plum.

2. Spray Yellow Salt over entire exterior surface. (This combination also works well in reverse, with a base coat of Yellow Salt and sprayed Purple Passion Plum.)

WILD WEST

1. Spray Strontium Crystal Magic at the top of the piece. Allow the glaze to build up in some areas.

2. Dip the pot four-fifths of the way up from the bottom of the piece in Ohata Khaki.

3. Pour Buttermilk in the interior of the piece and pour out.

4. Dip the top one-fourth of the piece in Buttermilk.

LIFE ON MARS *(Also shown on pages 38 and 39)*

1. Dip entire pot in Oxblood.

2. Spray The Juice, letting it build up in some areas, and feathering in others.

3. Pour Buttermilk across the piece.

4. (Optional) Dip Van Guilder Blue Ash at rim.

RAINBOW WATERFALL FOREST

(Also shown on the cover)

1. Spray The Juice at the top of the piece, allowing it to build up in some areas, and feathering others.

2. Dip the outside of the piece four-fifths of the way up in Reitz Green.

3. Pour Buttermilk on the inside of the piece and pour out, coating the entire interior.

4. Dip the top one-fourth of the piece in Buttermilk.

TUNDRA SUNSET *(Also shown on page 8)*

1. Dip the pot four-fifths of the way up from the bottom in Purple Passion Plum.

2. Pour Buttermilk on the inside of the piece and pour out, coating the entire interior.

3. Spray Strontium Crystal Magic at the top of the piece, allowing it to build up in some areas and feathering others.

4. (Optional) Dip Van Guilder Blue Ash at the rim.

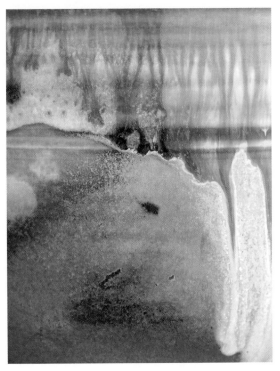

TROUBLESHOOTING

Even for experienced glaze artists, there are inevitably some stumbles along the way. Here are several of the problems you may encounter when glazing, and their solutions.

The tongs are leaving vampire bite marks: This can happen with any pair of tongs, and does not mean that your glaze needs adjusting. Wait until the coat of glaze has dried, then fill in the bare spots with a brush.

The clay body is showing through the glaze: The glaze is likely not dense enough. Increase the specific gravity, or submerge the piece in glaze for a longer period of time.

Glaze is cracking off the piece before firing: The glaze is too thick. The only remedy is to wash all the glaze off the pot, allow it to dry for 24 hours, and reglaze. Reduce the specific gravity of the layered glazes, or submerge the piece in glaze for a shorter period of time.

Unintentional glaze drips: You may get lucky, but these are almost always unattractive. Glaze drips can be avoided by inverting the piece over a bucket directly after removing it from the glaze. Wait until the piece stops dripping before inverting. If you do end up with any drips, you can smooth them out with a metal rib or burnish them with a gloved finger.

Not enough glaze is being absorbed on the second and third layers of a combination: Allow the piece to dry longer between coats, or use a fan to force-dry the surface. Never add a second or third coat of glaze until the layer below it has dried fully.

Coat of glaze is uneven: Make sure that the glaze has been stirred thoroughly so that it doesn't begin to settle out. You may need to do this every 3 to 4 minutes. Also, be sure to use a first-side-in-first-side-out technique for flatware, and invert vertical pieces after removing them from glaze.

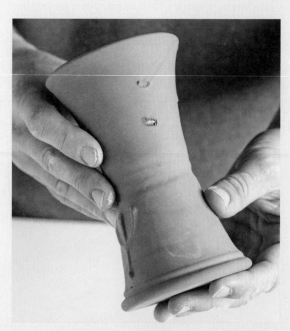

Cracking (top) is a sign that the glaze you applied is too thick. Vampire bite marks (bottom) are often unavoidable when using tongs, but they can be filled in.

GALLERY

Brushwork Platter. Sam Scott. *Photo courtesy of the artist.*

Confident brushwork divides the form but doesn't overcrowd it with information. Beautiful restraint is displayed by the artist.

Teabowl. Steven Hill. *Photo courtesy of the artist.*

The spray gun allows Steven Hill to layer his glazes, providing a smoother transition of colors and additional interaction between the amber and blue glazes. Notice the hints of green and yellow between the two glazes.

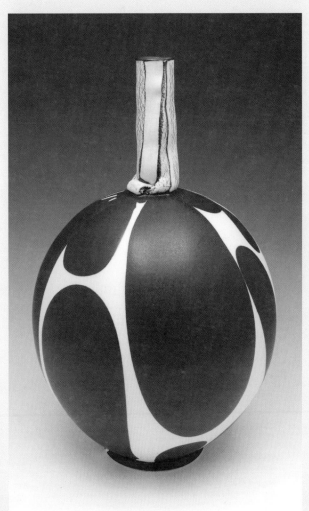

Black and White Vase with Handbuilt Neck. Sam Scott. *Photo courtesy of the artist.*

Sam Scott pours his glazes in a controlled manner. Each pour results in a rounded field of black glaze. The effect resembles river stones that have been smoothed down over the course of thousands of years.

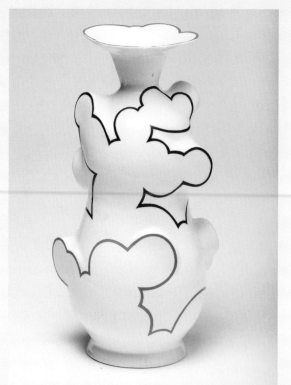

Garden Jug. Ben Carter. *Photo courtesy of the artist.*

The creamy, off-white glaze breaks nicely over the handle of the jug, revealing the red clay beneath. The curves of the all-around floral decoration are well-suited for this round pot.

Cloud Gourd Bottle. Sam Chung. *Photo courtesy of the artist.*

A high-gloss, smooth white background provides a clean look, while the red and black highlights accentuate the sculpted elements of this bottle.

UFO Vase. Nick Joerling. *Photo courtesy of the artist.*

The undulating line left by the corner of a rib is the perfect place to transition from one glaze to another in this vase.

Teapot. Deborah Schwartzkopf. *Photo courtesy of the artist.*

The use of a dark, matte glaze contrasted with a lighter, glossier glaze enhance the surface of this incredible teapot form.

Black Jar. Adrian Sandstrom. *Photo courtesy of the artist.*

The form and decoration of this piece work together to entice the viewer to contemplate it. You want to turn the piece around to see how it varies from side to side.

Black and White Teapot. Sam Scott. *Photo courtesy of the artist.*

Controlled pours of black glaze over white form teardrops that seemingly push up from the bottom and down from the top. This sense of movement reflects the manner in which the glaze was applied.

3

GOING FURTHER WITH GLAZE

It may take a kiln load or three to master those basic dance steps of glazing taught in Chapter 2. Having put in the time to master a set of glazes and glaze combinations, you may feel a sense of satisfaction—as well you should! Mastering glaze techniques, even the fundamentals, is no small feat. While it might be tempting to rest at the first feeling of contentment, I encourage you to continue the glaze journey with me. Examine the techniques in this chapter with an eye toward bringing additional variation and layers of expression to your work. Only through continued exploration will you discover never-before-seen combinations and colors and make your own contributions to the continuing evolution of the entire field of ceramics.

Variation and improvisation are personal processes that can work in perfect harmony with a more static body of work. Rather than feeling you must only stick to what you know or only experiment, instead think of the two as complementary. By establishing your own look with a set of glaze techniques, you create a launching pad for riffs and variations. If you want to make a dinnerware set, stick to what you know will work. However, if you are feeling inspired one weekend and have a few one-off mugs, it's time to set out on a new path of improvisation. Create variations on what you've been doing and see what shakes out in the firing. This sort of improvisation can help reflect who you are in the present moment. It allows you to show your personality, the particular way in which you relate to your chosen discipline and to the larger world.

BUILDING DEPTH

Let's start with some strategies for building depth in your surfaces. After all, one of the most common complaints for mid-range electric firings is that the surfaces are boring, lacking the depth of other firing methods, such as wood- and soda-firing (see a discussion of these methods on page 118). This is because an electric firing is a stable, neutral atmosphere that heats the glazes. That is, the firing itself adds nothing to what you have done to the surface of your work. Although it is by far the easiest way to fire your work, it is also the most challenging way to create visual interest on the surface of your piece. Thankfully, there are a number of ways to build depth and develop a more exciting look in an electric kiln.

Using incised lines and underglazes is a great way to build depth, as seen in this vase and cup by Laurie Caffery Harris.

The same glaze can look quite different depending on the clay body. Here, Odyssey Gloss White glaze is shown over a brown stoneware clay body (left) and a porcelain clay body (right).

One simple way to expand your palette with the same set of glazes you already use is to manipulate the color of the clay beneath the glazes. There are several ways to do this. First, you could use a different clay body. The same glaze will read very differently over dark brown stoneware than on porcelain or terra cotta. You can make test tiles in several kinds of clay to illustrate this point with your favorite glazes.

However, most clay artists tend to develop an affinity for a particular clay. They have a familiarity and appreciation for the clay's unique qualities. It just feels good to work with that clay. If you're at this point as well, that doesn't mean you're stuck with your favorite clay's color. Read on for a few interesting ways to alter the skin of your ceramic work to get the most out of your glazes, while still using the clay body you enjoy most.

SLIP, ENGOBES, AND TERRA SIGILLATA

Much like the candy coating of your favorite bite-size chocolate, slips, engobes, and terra sigillatas provide a thin layer of colored clay on the surface of your piece. A slip is essentially a liquid clay that you can make as thin or thick as you please. You can continue to use your favorite clay body, but coat some or all of your piece in a colored slip of your choosing to build depth. The glaze will respond to color of the slip, rather than the color of the clay beneath it. Partially coating a piece in slip will give you two different looks of the same glaze on the same piece.

You may want to mix a slip with a specific gravity of over 2.00 for an application like slip trailing, or as thin as 1.25 if you are dipping a piece in slip to coat it. While slips are generally applied when the clay is leather hard or bone dry, depending on the recipe and how much it shrinks in relation to the clay body, some recipes are formulated to be applied to bisqueware (see recipes on pages 190–192).

An engobe is similar to a slip, but with less clay and generally more silica. For this reason, engobes are usually glossier than slips, and can be applied on bisqueware. Note that all slip and engobe recipes should be screened as well.

Slips and engobes closely resemble glazes in their look and consistency before firing. Similarly, the application methods for applying glaze to a piece described in Chapter 2, and the alternative techniques described in this chapter, all represent viable techniques for applying slips and engobes. Getting creative with your application will add another layer of visual interest to your work and can help you develop your voice.

Slip trailing Ⓐ, brushing slip Ⓑ, pouring slip Ⓒ, and dipping in slip Ⓓ.

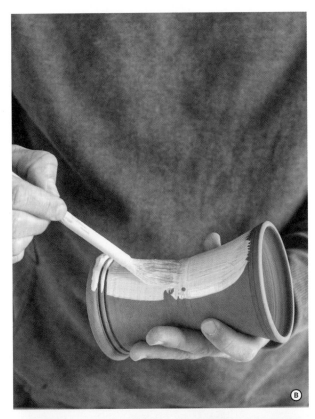

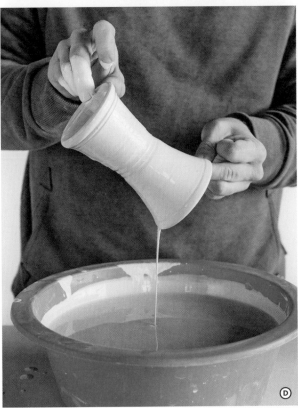

Terra sigillata, or "sealed earth," is a clay slip that has been refined to the point where it provides a glossy surface, especially when burnished. It can be used instead of or in addition to glaze. Terra sig, as it is known, is applied to bone-dry greenware and can be colored with oxides or mason stains, similar to a glaze. Cynthia Lee, a former director at Odyssey ClayWorks, uses terra sig on her beautiful low-fire, flora-inspired platters (see photo on page 72). To make terra sigillata, you will require just three ingredients: clay, water, and a deflocculant (a material that keeps a solution in suspension). You will also need some time for the process to take place. First, mix 10 grams defloculant, such as sodium silicate or Darvan 7, into 1 gallon of water. Add 2.5 pounds of clay (ball clay or Redart work well) and allow to settle overnight. When you return, the materials will have settled out into three distinct sections. Terra sigillata is the middle section and can be removed with a syringe. You can dispose of the sludgy lower section and thin top layer. You can then add colorant, if desired. (For recipe, see page 193.)

Wall Flower. Cynthia Lee. *Photo courtesy of the artist.*

The floral decoration neatly fills the interior surface of this platter by Cynthia Lee. Colored terra sigillatas provide a soft sheen.

Flower Cone. Cynthia Lee. *Photo courtesy of the artist.*

Terra sigillata combined with wire and beadwork bring this cone flower sculpture to life.

In these pieces by Naim Cash, black slip was applied and then carved through to reveal the white clay. The glaze is simply Odyssey Clear (page 173).

FISH SAUCE

The Odyssey studio has always stocked a mysterious and untraceable recipe for slip called Fish Sauce. This slip recipe is unique; not only is it easy to work with, it also has an enormous firing range. Unlike many slips, it can be fired to any common temperature, from cone 05 all the way up to cone 10. We tend to keep about four versions of Fish Sauce stocked at all times: the base recipe for white, plus black, green, and blue. Fish Sauce can be mixed thick for trailing, watered down and brushed on your work, or thinned even further for dipping.

Fish Sauce must be applied in the leather-hard state before the clay changes colors, or it may flake off while drying. The Fish Sauce recipes can be found on page 191. Additional color variations are possible using coloring oxides or mason stains as well. For a list of suggested additions of coloring oxides, see page 191.

Fish Sauce can be applied quite thick with a trailer, as shown on this pot, which has a black Fish Sauce design.

COMMERCIAL UNDERGLAZES

Commercial underglazes are carefully formulated combinations of clay and pigments that come in a variety of forms, including pencils, markers, watercolors, and oil pastels. However, they are most commonly bought and used by potters in a liquid, paintable medium that resembles a brightly colored slip. Underglazes are generally applied before (or under) a glaze, thus the name. However, underglazes can also be applied on top of glazes or between coats. While the recipes are generally not available, commercial underglazes come in an amazing array of different colors, including some very bright reds, oranges, and yellows, colors that are difficult to achieve for the average studio potter. Underglazes can be applied to clay in any state. They seem to absorb best into bone-dry greenware, yet applying them on bisque gives you the opportunity to wash off mistakes and combine underglazes with resist techniques (see page 79).

Commercial underglazes in liquid form are usually applied by brush and require two to three coats in order to be opaque. When

Commercial underglazes need not be applied thick, straight out of the jars. Laurie Caffery Harris uses them in a more painterly fashion, as seen on this plate.

brushing, make sure to let the base coat dry thoroughly before adding another layer. Underglazes do not run, which makes them popular for doing any kind of detailed illustrations.

Just as with slip, the use of underglazes beneath your glaze can result in many new variations on a single glaze. Try making a test piece with several different colors of underglaze, then add a single coat of glaze, and witness how you have created several new looks for the same glaze.

Washes and stains are often sponged off after application, which can highlight elements of a piece.

Green Whiskey Cup. Micah Thanhauser.
Photo courtesy of the artist.

Blue Whiskey Cup. Micah Thanhauser.
Photo courtesy of the artist.

A wash of copper on one bowl and cobalt on the other illustrate the effect an underlying color can have on the glaze above it. Each piece was glazed with Gen's Satin Matte, recipe on page 174.

WASHES OR STAINS

Washes, also called stains, are coloring oxides suspended in water, sometimes with the addition of a little clay or frit (a manufactured prefired glaze) to help them bond to the surface of a pot. Washes are very powerful, and as such they are often applied and then washed off with a damp sponge to reveal some of the clay body below. This can leave more oxide in lower-lying areas, such as carvings, and it consequently gently colors the higher area, accentuating any decorative elements. Washes can also be used to affect the color applied above it, an effect particularly noticeable in the crystalline glazed whiskey cups made by Micah Thanhauser, shown above. Washes are applied to bisqueware, but you can also experiment with painting them on top of glaze, which is referred to as glaze painting, or overglaze. This generally creates more movement on the surface than when the wash is applied underneath. You can find wash recipes on page 193.

RESISTS

One of the overarching themes of this book is to get just the right amount of glaze on your piece exactly where you want it. But what do you do when there's a part of your pot where you don't want glaze? It's time to look at different types of resists.

Don't be afraid to try combinations of these resist techniques to bring additional depth, imagery, and color to your work. For example, you could combine sticker, tape, stencil, and freehand waxing in the same piece to accentuate their interplay, each giving a different quality of line; hard and angular, curved and flowing, concrete or abstract. You will soon find a style that others find irresistible.

Resists were used on these rectangular platters by the author to define the white areas.

WAX

There are several commercially produced wax resists. Forbes wax and Aftosa wax are water-based waxes. They flow naturally off a brush and are quite versatile. Mobil resist, which can be hard to find these days as it is out of production, is petroleum-based, slightly thicker than the Forbes and Aftosa wax, and reliable, though it is less suited for decorative work, as its thickness doesn't allow it to flow quite as well off the brush. All these waxes will need time to cure to function most effectively. Wait at least 15 minutes, or until the sheen has gone away, before glazing. An hour is better, and if you are using wax resist brushwork as decoration, wait overnight. These waxes can be hard to see when applied to bisque, as they dry a matte clear, so it can be a good idea to dye them with food coloring, making it much easier to see where you have waxed and where you have not waxed. (Aftosa wax comes precolored.) Add ten to twenty drops of food coloring to a gallon of wax to tint. The dendritic expansion of food coloring into wax is one of those moments in the glaze kitchen that always puts a smile on my face. (Remember to enjoy not just the finished results, but the process as well.)

Any glaze left on the bottom of the piece will fuse your work to the kiln shelf during firing, damaging either your work or the shelf. You may want to wax ¼ inch up the side of the foot as well, particularly when using runny glazes. Some people use a combination of paraffin and beeswax that is heated to the melting point on an electric pancake griddle. You can cover the bottom of a large piece quickly with this method, but this wax is not suitable for brushing. When you're using this method, do so in a well-ventilated area, and make sure to turn the griddle off when you are done, as this heated material is a fire hazard. If you accidentally get wax where you don't want it, you can get it out with 90 percent rubbing alcohol, available in most pharmacies, or you can rebisque the work.

Most artists use wax to keep glaze from sticking to the bottom of their pots.

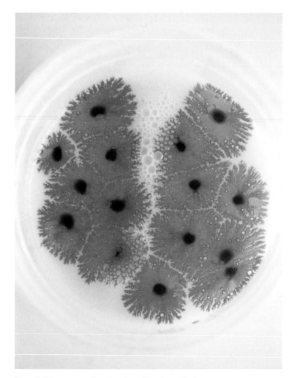

Dendritic expansion is visually stunning.

Yunomi. Michael Kline. *Photo courtesy of Tim Barnwell.*

Yunomi. Michael Kline. *Photo courtesy of Tim Barnwell.*

The stamped decoration is contrasted with the wax resist brushwork in this Yunomi by Michael Kline (no relation to the author). Coloring oxides have been added to the wax.

WAX FOR LIDS

To keep lids from sticking to pots during firing, try adding a little bit of alumina hydrate (one of the main ingredients in kiln wash) to your wax. A teaspoon per cup of wax should suffice. Apply this wax to the places where the lid meets the pot before glazing and firing.

Waxes that are applied over bisque will burn off in the firing, leaving the clay body exposed. This can be a dramatic effect, particularly when you are using a clay body that fires to an attractive color that complements and contrasts with the glaze. Remember, though: you do not want to expose the clay body on the food-bearing surfaces of functional work.

Wax can be used in even more creative ways. For example, consider applying it on top of a coat of glaze when layering. The second coat of glaze will absorb everywhere except for the waxed areas, exposing the first coat of glaze below. Or perhaps you want to paint a design on your piece with underglazes, apply clear glaze on top, and wax that portion of the pot. Then when you dip the entire pot in a colored glaze, the wax will keep the glaze off your decoration. Finally, you can add coloring oxides or mason stains to the wax, providing additional coloring to your brushwork; a teaspoon per pint is a good place to start.

Note: Wax can ruin brushes. Make sure you either rinse out your brush extremely well after using wax, or use a dedicated wax brush kept in water while not in use. A brush with wax left in it will quickly stiffen so much that it will become unusable.

Since you can peel latex off after it has cured, you have additional opportunities to layer glaze.

LATEX

Liquid latex is another type of resist. It has a pungent smell, but it can be worth the olfactory annoyance. Latex has a unique quality: it can be peeled off once it has cured. This allows you to lay down your resists either on bisque or on top a layer of glaze, add a (second) coat of glaze, and then peel off the latex. This process can raise dust from the glaze though, so be sure to wear a mask when you try this technique. The resisted area can then receive an additional coat of glaze, if desired. With the wax resists, the area of the resist can receive no more material once cured as nothing else will stick. Latex allows you to return to glazing the resisted area.

TAPE

Many different tapes can be used to resist underglaze, washes, and glazes. Painter's tape, artist's tape, and masking tape all work well. Masking tape can be found in art stores, hardware stores, and online in a number of different thicknesses, ranging from ⅛ inch to 2½ inches. If you like to work with line imagery, or hard, angular geometry, tape resists will give you a truer line than trying to freehand it with a brush. Once you have your tape in place, run your finger over it to smooth it and seal the edges. It is possible that some glaze will migrate under the edge of the tape, but this can be cleaned up with a needle tool or stylus once you remove the tape. You can also cut the tape with an X-ACTO knife while it's on the pot to create custom designs. For an excellent example of the power of tape, see Molly Morning-glory and Naim Cash's pieces on pages 113 and 114.

Apply a sticker, apply glaze, then carefully remove the sticker for a precise resist with some of the upside of latex.

STICKERS

Like tape resist, stickers can be placed on bisque or glazed surfaces to resist the next coat of glaze. An enormous amount of design work has already been done by the sticker manufacturer, but you can also customize your own stickers. Sticker paper is available at most office supply stores. You can sketch your designs on the paper, then use scissors or a craft knife to cut them out. As with tape resists, be sure to smooth the stickers down before glazing. You may need to go back and clean up the lines if any glaze was able to migrate underneath the surface of the sticker.

Commercial stencils are an easy way to transfer imagery to a piece.

STENCILS

Stencils made from paper or plastic can be used to create additional imagery when decorating or glazing. Stencil film, which is an adhesive vinyl, also works well. An enormous number of commercial stencils are available, or you can make your own custom designs. Stencils work best when brushing or spraying, and you can affix them to your piece using artist's tape.

CHAPTER 3

Anja Bartels and the Plastic Wrap Resist Technique

Using plastic wrap instead of wax was the key for Anja's clean surfaces. It might work for you as well.

Originally from Hamburg, Germany, stencil artist Anja Bartels discovered pottery making while living in an intentional community in Virginia. Passion ignited, she returned home to study in the German Ceramics Guild, which honed her skills in a way much different from the typical experience in American art schools. With a strong focus on craftsmanship and technical skill, Guild training provided her with the groundwork for making a high-quality product paired with the practical experience of working with a master potter for three years. Guild apprentices must engage in all aspects of the business, including marketing, sales, accounting, and production.

Anja's nautically themed porcelain employs several different techniques including slip trailing and sgraffito (a technique in which underglaze is painted onto greenware and a design is carved back through, revealing the clay body underneath). She pours and sprays glazes, using a unique resist technique for some pieces, such as the beautiful urchin bowl seen here. She throws and trims these bowls on the wheel, then applies several thousand small slip-trailed spikes using a surgical bulb while she listens to audiobooks about shipwrecks. Anja's personal aesthetic and process are consistent and highly developed, reflecting her upbringing in a port town and her

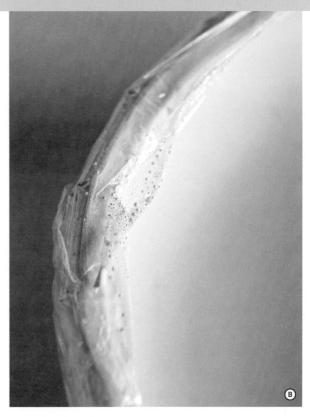

love of ships and the sea. After bisque firing, Anja glazes only the inside of the bowls by first pouring Chun Celadon (page 171) into the inside of the piece, then spraying Strontium Crystal Magic (page 179) onto the interior. The exterior surface is left bare, showcasing the beautiful white porcelain clay and slip decoration.

When glazing, Anja first carefully pours the celadon glaze to coat only the interior of the piece. Then, to keep any glaze from running onto the outside of the piece, which is covered in thousands of spikes and would be a nightmare to properly wax, Anja tightly wraps the outside, spiky surface with plastic wrap and seals it with artist's tape. Ⓐ

Then she sprays the second glaze, removes the plastic wrap and tape, and cleans with a sponge any places where the glaze migrated under the tape. Ⓑ The result is dynamic, contrasting the smooth, watery blue glaze with the hardened white surface of the unglazed porcelain. It is as if these pieces were born in the sea. Ⓒ

Urchin Bowl. Anja Bartels.
Photo courtesy of Laurie Caffery Harris.

A completed urchin bowl. The plastic wrap resist has prevented any glaze from marring the pure-white porcelain exterior.

Sailing Ships Platter. Anja Bartels.
Photo courtesy of Laurie Caffery Harris.

Sgraffito decoration and gold decals fill the interior of this handbuilt porcelain platter. The slip-trailed rim is left unglazed, showcasing the beauty of the porcelain.

Urchin Luminary. Anja Bartels.
Photo courtesy of Laurie Caffery Harris.

The candle on the inside of this luminary reflects the celadon glaze on its interior and casts an ethereal blue light through the carved decoration.

Peacock Teapot. Anja Bartels.
Photo courtesy of Laurie Caffery Harris.

The sgraffito tree is carved in black underglaze onto the bone dry porcelain teapot.

After bisque firing, Odyssey Clear (page 173) glaze is applied and fired to cone 7. The gold luster and peacock decal are then applied and fired to cone 018. More to come on decals and lusters in Chapter 4.

ALTERNATIVE APPLICATION TECHNIQUES

The basic glazing techniques of dipping, pouring, brushing, trailing, and spraying you acquired in Chapter 2 are by no means the only ways to apply glaze to a piece. I learned this lesson long ago, but recently my daughter, Stella Ro, reminded me of it. She has been coming with me to the studio since she was born, and she began making her own work at the age of two. She has always been fascinated by the material, and one of her favorite activities is to "play clay." Stella Ro's playful approach to tools and materials has opened my eyes to ways of working that I never would have thought of.

One day, while we were glazing some of her work, Stella Ro opened a tool bin, grabbed a spoon and asked, "Dada, spoon?" While it had not occurred to me to use a spoon to apply glaze to a piece, I smiled at her and told her, "Sure." She carefully took a spoonful of glaze out of the bucket, gently pouring it onto a texturized, bisque-fired slab she had made. There was a certain grace to the movement, and the glaze laid out in a manner that would not have been possible in any other way. It opened my eyes to the fact that anything could be used to apply glaze: a chopstick, a wrench, a feather, a tire iron. I encourage you to improvise, to experiment with found materials, or to make your own applicators. In this way, you will begin to develop your own process that is unique to the way you work, resulting in decorative patterns that have never been seen before.

LADLING GLAZE

Porcelain glazers in Jingdezhen, China, have a unique and beautiful way of glazing the inside of a bowl. The bowl is held upside down over a large vat of glaze. Using a ladle and with a quick, efficient flick of the wrist, the glaze is thrown upward from the ladle into the inside of the bowl. The impact of the glaze spreads it out over the interior surface of the bowl as the excess runs and drips back into the vat. It is a practiced move, requiring both skill and repetition to master, but may be the most efficient way to glaze the interior of a bowl—an important consideration when glazing hundreds, if not thousands of bowls in a day. Ladling can also be used for more decorative glazing designs.

With some practice, you too can ladle glaze!

SPONGING

Glazes may be sponged onto the surface of a pot or onto an existing layer of glaze. Sponging allows the glaze to spread unevenly because of the porosity of the sponge, and it can be a great way to create a misty look with the applied glaze. Sponges may also be cut into custom designs using scissors or an X-ACTO knife to leave concrete imagery in glaze.

DRY GLAZING

Glazes in their dry, mixed form may be sprinkled through a handheld kitchen strainer, like putting powdered sugar on pancakes. This works best on horizontal surfaces, as the glaze rests on top of the surface, rather than penetrating it. Be sure to wear a dust mask or respirator whenever you are dry glazing, and be sure to work in a ventilated spray booth or outdoors. Be very careful when transporting this work and loading the kiln, as the glaze materials are resting on top of the piece and are easily disturbed.

SPECIAL CONSIDERATIONS

Some pieces you create may require special techniques or equipment to successfully glaze them. Large pieces that won't fit in a bucket, small pieces that cannot be held with tongs, and delicate pieces all require a special approach.

GLAZING LARGE WORK

For work that is larger than any bucket or pebble bowl you may have, there are still several ways to get an even coat of glaze. These techniques require more than one person, so don't be afraid to ask a friend for help.

To glaze the interior of a large vertical piece, pour several pitchers of glaze into the inside of the piece. Station an assistant next to the work with a large container to catch the excess glaze as you pour it out. Quickly but smoothly pick up the piece and begin to rotate it to coat the entire interior of the vessel. As you are turning it, invert it to the point where it begins to pour out of the neck. Try to make two full revolutions to coat the entire interior, then pour out all the excess glaze. The water in the glaze will begin to permeate the entire piece from the inside, so you may see discoloration from the outside. For this reason, wait until the next day, when the water has evaporated out of the bisque, to glaze the exterior of the piece. Otherwise, the saturated bisque will absorb insufficient glaze, yielding an unintended and often unsatisfactory result.

Once the interior glaze has dried, place the large piece on a banding wheel sitting inside a large pebble bowl, either right-side up or inverted, depending on the degree of a glaze's runniness. Inverted will work better for runny glazes, as more glaze will build up at the top of the pieces. Excessive runny glaze at the bottom of a large piece risks its loss as it is much easier for the glaze to flow off the piece and fuse it to the kiln shelf below. If the lip of the piece is narrower than the width of the banding wheel, you may want to place the piece on two equally thick pieces of wood so that the glaze can flow off the lip of the piece without building up too much. If pouring, spin the banding wheel slowly, pouring glaze from the top of the piece while it spins. The glaze will run down the side of the pot and flow off the lip. Let the banding wheel make two full revolutions before pouring the glaze lower down on the piece. Continue pouring glaze down the piece until the entire exterior is coated. Wait until the piece has dried to remove from the banding wheel.

While pouring glaze over large work is the quickest way to cover the surface with glaze, you can also spray the surface, or use brushes. Dipping is possible, but requires several people, containers the size of a bathtub or larger, and massive (100,000-gram) batches of glaze.

Large horizontal pieces, such as platters or wide-rimmed bowls, present a different set of challenges. The inside of the piece is generally the focus with low, wide forms, and they are rarely amenable to the pouring technique described above: too much glaze will pool up in the interior of the piece, causing bubbling in the glaze when fired. Although you will need a large batch of glaze to fill it, a kiddie pool filled with glaze can make for straightforward, easy dipping, again utilizing the first-side-in-first-side-out technique described in Chapter 2. You may also choose to brush or spray glaze onto large horizontal forms.

If you want to dip larger pieces, make sure you have a large enough container for glaze and have a clear plan for how you will execute the dip.

For very large work, you will either need to spray or pour your glaze.

GLAZING SMALL WORK

Traditional tools such as channel lock tongs may not work well for glazing very small work. You may need to improvise or make your own tools to suit the tiny scale. You can use a pair of tweezers for dipping or holding a piece while you pour glaze over it. For brushing, you may want to cut the bristles of a small brush as far down as a single strand. When spraying, the wind created by the compressed, aerated glaze can easily knock over a tiny piece. Use some white glue (Elmer's or similar) to affix the piece to a bisque-fired cookie to anchor it. Wait until the glue has set up before glazing.

Note: Many people have amazing collections of tiny ceramic art. Jon Almeda has carved out a beautiful niche in the world of miniatures, and his work is highly collected.

GLAZING DELICATE WORK

Very thin work, or work with very fine detail, needs to be handled carefully. Tongs can easily crack the porous bisque, especially once submerged in glaze. Use a pair of gloved hands instead. Should a piece of bisque crack while you are glazing, be sure to screen the glaze immediately to make sure any broken bisque shards are removed. The only thing worse than breaking one piece is to have the remnants of that piece stick to your next piece and ruin that one as well.

Glazing small work presents its own challenges!

GALLERY

Chubby Unicorn Pride.
Mac Star McCusker.
Photo courtesy of the artist.

A rainbow of underglaze on its horn transforms this rhino into a "Chubby Unicorn" and provides an additional visual statement.

Bowl with Handles. Nick Joerling. *Photo courtesy of the artist.*

A single brushstroke of wax resist on the exterior of this bowl provides a third color and textures in this thrown and altered bowl.

Serving Platter. Sara Ballek. *Photo courtesy of Halima Flynt.*

Brightly colored underglazes enliven the surface of this wheel-thrown and pinched platter.

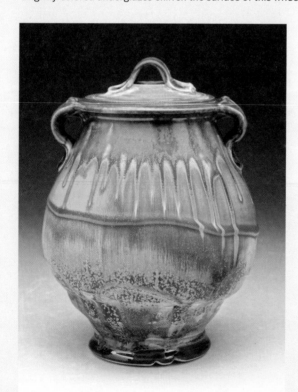

Covered Jar. Steven Hill. *Photo courtesy of the artist.*

Layered glazes run beautifully down the side of the pot, cascading over the slip decoration on this magnificent jar. Truly amazing glaze.

Cloud Flask. Sam Chung. *Photo courtesy of the artist.*

Underglaze stays put when applied, as can be seen in the sharp black line of the cloud on this bottle.

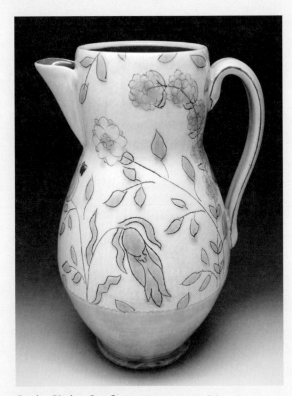

Garden Pitcher. Ben Carter. *Photo courtesy of the artist.*

The glaze used to color the leaves and flowers gently bleeds through the incised decoration, giving a soft, pleasant aesthetic to this pitcher.

Cabin Vase. Laurie Caffery Harris. *Photo courtesy of the artist.*

The imagery is first carved into the pot using an X-ACTO knife, then filled in with a wash. Then the entire surface is sponged, which leaves color only in the incised lines. Underglaze watercolors are used to color the piece.

Contrasting Swans. Taylor Robenalt. *Photo courtesy of the artist.*

Boldly colored underglazes and lusters (covered in the next chapter) bring additional life to these exquisitely executed porcelain sculptures.

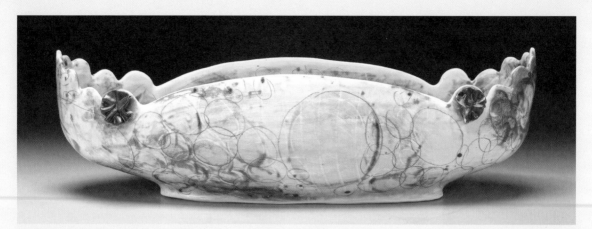

"Sophie" Serving Bowl. Angelique Tassistro. *Photo courtesy of the artist.*

A top coat of clear glaze showcases underglaze that has been applied and wiped away, and the fine lines applied with an underglaze pencil.

Push Play. Sam Scott. *Photo courtesy of the artist.*

Brightly colored underglazes jump off this platter.

Serving Dishes. Deborah Schwartzkopf. *Photo courtesy of the artist.*

I am intrigued by the small amount of contrasting color on the handle of these elongated bowls.

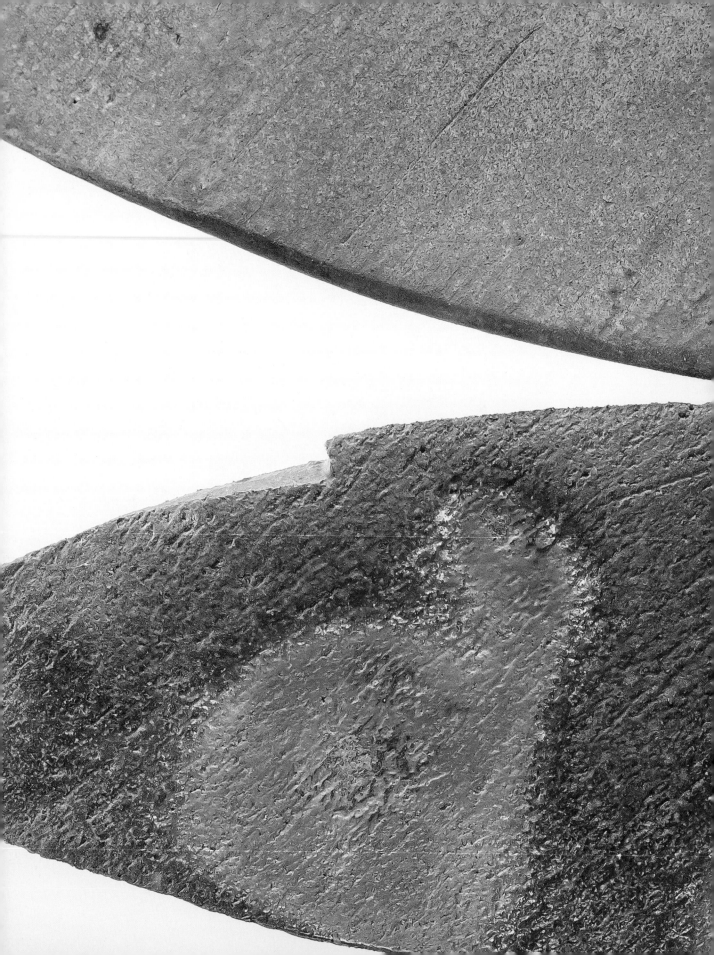

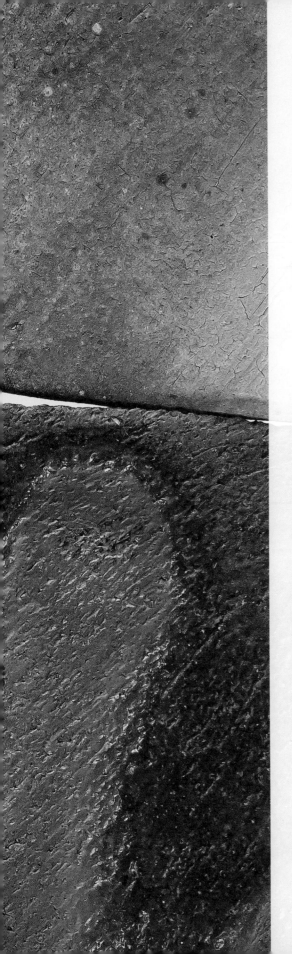

4

SPECIAL TOPICS

The Japanese say it takes ten years to master the skill of centering clay. Not just to center at its most basic, but to do it masterfully, with grace. All master craftspeople follow similar yet individual paths. First, as students of a craft, they copied the masters who came before them. They became completely absorbed in their craft, developing competence in the basic techniques. They then began to improvise, and in so doing discovered their own voices. With repetition, dedication, and passion, they created something new, memorable, and of undeniable artistic merit. In this chapter, we will explore several special topics with masterful glaze artists who have established themselves within modern American ceramics.

While many of the techniques you'll find in this chapter take time to perfect—including plenty of trial and error—I encourage you to spend the time required to master what speaks to you. If you are aiming for high levels of achievement in your ceramic work, don't let the perfect become the enemy of the good. Instead, build upon the good over time, and as you become technically competent, allow yourself to experiment and improvise. Try something new, and see what calls to you!

REDS

There is an old adage for success in the ceramic arts: "Make it good. And if you can't make it good, make it big. And if you can't make it big, paint it red." Perhaps this maxim exists because the psychological impact of the color red is one of the most intense on the spectrum. Yet if you know potters, they'll also tell you it's because both chemistry and physics make it difficult to get a good red in the kiln. There are challenges sourcing materials, some of which are rare and occasionally toxic (such as lead and uranium). Other materials are quite expensive and must be carefully fired to avoid burning out. Thus, red pieces (and similarly purple, orange, and pink ones) have a certain mystery and power to them.

TIN/CHROME REDS

Tin/chrome reds produce off-red tones, such as mulberry and maroon, that are often quite beautiful. I've found that the combination of the colorants tin oxide and chrome oxide in oxidation can result in a range of colors, from pink to plum. Tin/chrome reds require very exact mixing, as most recipes require just a pinch (as little as 0.5 percent chrome oxide and maybe as much as 5 percent tin oxide). In order to ensure that these glazes perform well, make sure to measure carefully! Fat Cat Red (recipe on page 172) is an excellent example of a tin/chrome red at cone 6. Fat Cat Red plays well with others, including Chun Celadon, and provides a nice base glaze that doesn't run. For a truer red, I recommend using a copper red in reduction, or an encapsulated red glaze.

The Radiant Red underglaze provides the pop of red you see here. The base glaze is Chun Celadon.

COPPER REDS

In reduction, especially at cone 10, copper can produce a beautiful *sang de boeuf*, or oxblood red. Copper reds are finicky, requiring technical mastery—and sometimes they're still elusive. Entire books have been written dedicated to these remarkable glazes, the best of which is Robert Tichane's *Copper Red Glazes*. In brief, copper reds must be fired carefully, as too much reduction and heat will burn out all the red, leaving a gray or clear glaze, and too little will result in an equally unattractive green-tinted finish. With copper reds, it is important both to get enough glaze onto the pot (generally 2 to 3 millimeters, but careful: too much can cause the glaze to run) and to nail the amount of reduction at just the right time. I recommend starting reduction between cone 012 and cone 010, continuing up to cone 04. It may take several firings to get it just right, but when you do, the results are spectacular. Oxblood and Purple Passion Plum (recipes on page 163 and 169) are great copper red glazes. See the sample firing schedule on page 142.

ENCAPSULATED REDS

Cadmium oxide is a highly toxic material that can produce brilliant yellows, oranges, and reds when fired to ceramic temperatures. In order to overcome the dangerous nature of this material, labs "encapsulate" cadmium in a zirconium sphere, rendering it inert and therefore chemically preventing it from leaching out of the glaze. While expensive (the cost is reflected in the price of encapsulated stains and glaze), encapsulated cadmium underglazes and glazes provide some of the most vivid and powerful colors available to the ceramic artist. Commercially produced Christmas Red and Fire Engine Red glazes often incorporate encapsulated cadmium oxide. The Radiant Red trailer, described on page 51 is a prime example of the potency of encapsulated cadmium oxide as well. The material is available to the studio potter in the form of encapsulated mason stains and Cerdec/Degussa stains. While encapsulated reds are a splurge, they can bring a vibrancy to your work unattainable by any other method.

Red Bottle. Adrian Sandstrom. *Photo courtesy of the artist.*

Encapsulated reds provide the brightest examples of the color in ceramics, as in this dynamic pot.

CRYSTALLINE GLAZES

Humans have been fascinated with crystals throughout our history. Crystals form when certain molecules align in a lattice formation that is uniform and repeated. In nature, crystals can take millions of years to form. Crystals can also be produced in a lab—and, to our delight, by a studio potter in the kiln.

Crystalline glazes require the presence of zinc oxide, silica, and titanium dioxide to create crystals in the surface of the glaze. The three combine to form a zinc-silicate crystal, but the right conditions have to exist in order for them to do so. The titanium nuclei represent the "seeds" of the crystal, which will then grow in a sea of silica and zinc. Most of the time, the glaze, made predominantly from Ferro Frit 3110 and other low-fire ingredients, will be overfired to cone 6 or 10 to create a flowing medium in which the seed crystals float. The temperature will then be lowered and held in order for the crystals to grow, but precautions must be taken to capture the excess flowing glaze. To do this, crystalline potters often throw a separate porcelain drip tray that sits below the piece itself. Grinding is a way of life for the crystalline potter, but with the right tools, the process is fairly simple. (See page 145 for an examination of diamond sanding tools and techniques.)

MICRO VERSUS MACRO CRYSTALS

A number of glazes will naturally produce small (micro) crystals up to 2 millimeters in the course of a normal firing, including Strontium Crystal Magic, The Juice, and Gen's Satin Matte (recipes on pages 179, 163, and 174, respectively). These glazes are either self-decorating (Gen's Satin Matte) or can provide the addition of small crystals when layered over or under another glaze (Strontium Crystal Magic and The Juice, although both of these glazes look terrible when used alone).

If you are after larger crystals, I recommend using glazes specifically formulated to promote the growth of large crystals. These glazes are generally high in Ferro Frit 3110, zinc oxide, silica, titanium dioxide, and colorants with very little clay. Additionally, use a firing program at cone 10 with several long holds on the way down in order to give the crystals the most time to develop. Most crystalline potters "soak" the kiln for 3 to 5 hours between 1,850 and 2,100 degrees Fahrenheit as the kiln is cooling down. Growing large crystals in a kiln is an energy- and labor-intensive endeavor, and crystalline potters experience a very high loss rate, although some pieces may be saved through refiring. While the payoff is tremendous, as in the stunning piece by Frank Vickery on page 125, the pursuit is not for the faint of heart!

Nick Moen's crystalline glaze produces large crystals. See pages 102 and 103 for more information on this unique glaze.

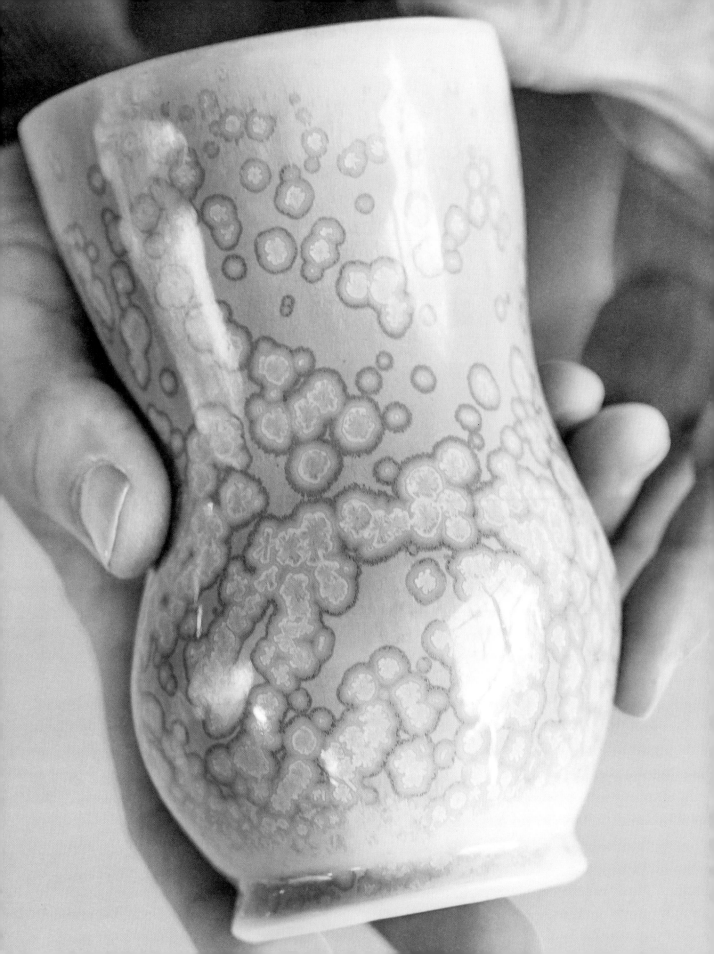

Unique Crystalline with Nick Moen and Genevieve Van Zandt

Nick Moen (cups at left) and Genevieve Van Zandt (sculpture at right) developed the Gen's Satin Matte recipe together, then took it in different directions to suit their work.

In the firmament of young American ceramic artists, Nick Moen and Genevieve Van Zandt are bright, shining stars. From Minneapolis, Minnesota, and Detroit, Michigan, respectively, these two Midwesterners were studio mates at Odyssey in 2014. In some ways, their styles could not contrast more. Nick's work has focused on sleekly designed forms to be slip cast. His work is modern, urban, refined, understated, and quietly beautiful. Upon examination, Genevieve's work offers a phantasmagorical appreciation of a natural world that opens onto mystical possibilities. The yin-and-yang nature of their friendship formed the basis for some truly entertaining collaborations that resulted in interesting advancements in the studio.

One Nick-and-Genevieve collaboration saw the development of a new glaze, as well as a new fast-fire crystalline technique that saved both energy and time while forming beautiful crystals at cone 6. The story of the development of this glaze illustrates several interesting qualities regarding the nature of matte glazes.

Both artists sought an alternative to the glossy nature of most of the Odyssey house glazes, so they set out to develop a satin matte glaze that could add range to the textural possibilities in the glaze recipe. The result was Gen's Satin Matte (see recipe on page 179). Genevieve colored the base glaze with a variety of bright mason stains, and thereby created a seven-color rainbow. She brushed the glazes onto her sculpted porcelain, which achieved a lovely, gloss-free, vibrant surface distinct from so many of the other glazes that were being used at the time.

Nick used this same glaze on the surfaces of his slip-cast porcelain line. Preparing for an upcoming show, Nick managed to fill one extra kiln the night

Crash Cool Copper Glaze detail. Nick Moen. *Photo courtesy of the artist.*

Detail shot of microcrystals on the surface of a pillow platter.

before leaving. In order to get the work to cool in time to be displayed, he fast-fired the kiln, and when it reached temperature, he "crash-cooled" it by opening the lid of the kiln (using gloves and protective gear), reducing the heat from the top temperature to just above quartz inversion (1,100 degrees Fahrenheit).

This happened at around 4:00 a.m. Returning to open the kiln at 7:00 a.m., Nick found that his pots were covered in beautiful, dime-size crystals. The whole firing had taken less than 10 hours to heat up to cone 6 and cool to room temperature. How was this possible? It turns out that many matte to semigloss or satin matte glazes are the result of microcrystals that cover the entire surface of the piece. Genevieve's mason-stained, rainbow version of Gen's Satin Matte is an example of this. In Nick's firing, however, the crystals had begun to form, but were frozen before they could meet each other and form a matte surface. Instead, there are matte crystals suspended in a glossier background, but produced in one-quarter of the time and at a lower temperature than traditional crystalline glazing, obviating the additional step of grinding the bases of the pots. Necessity being the mother of invention, Nick's haste resulted in a new approach to the glaze, with a dynamic and unexpected result.

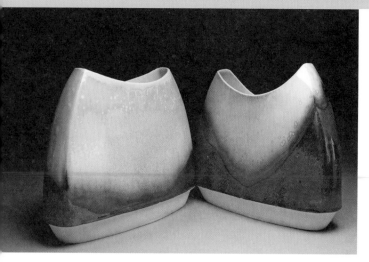

Envelope Vases. Nick Moen. *Photo courtesy of the artist.*

This glaze provides a variety of colors, even in the areas that don't grow as many crystals.

Waffle Mugs. Nick Moen. *Photo courtesy of the artist.*

The charcoal glazes at the bottom of these mugs slows the flow of the crystalline glazes at the top, preventing them from running off of the foot.

Drinking Vases. Nick Moen. *Photo courtesy of the artist.*

Slip casting provides regularity of form, but the crystal development gives each piece in the set an individual look.

Roses and Thorns. Genevieve Van Zandt. *Photo courtesy of the artist.*

Glazed porcelain flora, fauna, and minerals combine in harmony to create this wall hanging.

Floragasmic Explosion. Genevieve Van Zandt. *Photo courtesy of the artist.*

Mason stains can be used to color a base glaze to offer the artist an expanded palette.

DECALS, CHINA PAINTS, AND LUSTERS

Glaze myth #818: The glaze fire is the end of the road.

After the initial glaze firing, many people think that the piece is finished and unable to be altered further. Disappointing or boring pots may be sold as seconds, given as gifts, or hidden from sight. However, this belief is far from the truth. Multiple glaze firings can both take care of glaze faults and add more visual interest to your piece. Many potters rely on this technique to build up the surface of their work, including John Tilton, Adrian Saxe, and Eric Knoche. (For a discussion of refiring, see page 146.) A dull pot can also be turned up through the addition of printed images, precious metals, or painted imagery in a third—or fourth or fifth—firing. Three interrelated decorating methods—decals, lusters, and china paints—are terrific options to add depth, meaning, and visual interest to your glazed ware. These processes require a third firing, often to a much lower temperature, but will not undo any of the work you have already done.

DECALS

Decals are commercially produced for sale in a great variety of colors and designs. If you have access to a color ceramic decal printer, you can also print your own decals in almost any color. However, these color ceramic decal printers are expensive, running north of $5,000. Thankfully, several companies, including Milestone Decal Art, will print custom decals for you—even if you need just a single sheet.

Julia Claire Weber's work explores the possibilities of artist-designed decals. See more of her process on pages 110 and 111.

If you can be satisfied with sepia or dark brown–toned monochromes, there's another way to print and use nearly any image you can bring up on your computer. The only trick is finding one of several inexpensive printers that utilize red iron oxide and manganese dioxide in their ink.

- HP LaserJet M1212nf MFP

- HP LaserJet 4L

- HP LaserJet 5L

- HP P1005 LaserJet

- HP P1006 LaserJet

- Printers that accept HP LaserJet print cartridge 12A or 85A

Using specialty decal paper, you can print and apply images to the side of your glazed piece, and fire to witness cone 04. To apply most decals:

1. Always clean the surface of your piece before applying a decal, as dust and dirt can cause the image to peel. A paper towel moistened with a little bit of rubbing alcohol works well.

2. The decals will be printed on decal paper, which has a clear plastic topcoat that contains the image, on top of a thick stabilizer paper. In order to separate the two so that your decal can be applied to your work, first cut out the design and place it in a bowl of water. Ⓐ

3. After approximately 1 minute, the decal will be ready for application. First, line up where you want to put your decal. Then, using the backing paper for stability, slide the decal off the paper and into place on your work, ink side down. Ⓑ

Ⓐ

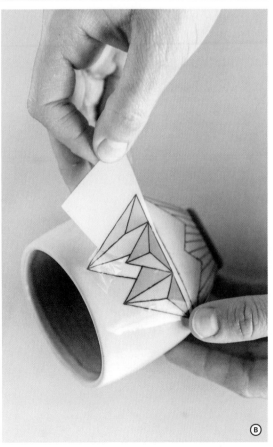

Ⓑ

(C)

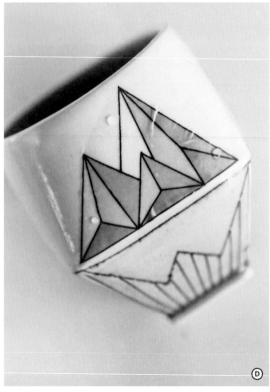

(D)

4. Use a paper towel or sponge to squeeze moisture out from the inside to the edges. Be gentle. If you are too abrasive, you can tear through the design. Try to get as much moisture as possible out from under the image. ⓒ

5. Allow the piece to dry. Place carefully in the kiln and fire to the cone suggested by the manufacturer. ⓓ

Note: You want to be careful with decal imagery, as many images you'll find online have been trademarked.

CHINA PAINTS

China paints are applied directly onto the surface of the glazed work and fired to cone 018. They are commercially produced and available in a rainbow of colors. China painting is a highly specialized pursuit, although certainly anyone can try it. China paints are made by combining coloring oxides with a small amount of lead oxide frits and mixing in a bit of oil. They are widely available through ceramic suppliers.

Much like oil painting, china painting requires a steady hand, as it is very difficult to remove paint if you get it where you don't want it. As with decals, be sure to clean the piece before beginning. The china paints can be applied as you would paint on a canvas, but make sure you know what image you want to create before you begin painting. China paints are unforgiving and smear when you try to wipe them off. You've only got one shot to get it right! Additionally, use care and handle the piece only where there is no china paint to avoid finger marks and smudges before firing. Because of the petroleum base, fire the pots in a well-ventilated kiln. (As an interesting side note, color decals designed for ceramics are printed using china paints.)

LUSTERS

The addition of precious metals to artwork always increases its perceived value. The psychological impact on the viewer is undeniable. Gold! Silver! Platinum! We equate these materials with wealth and status. It is possible to fire precious metals directly onto your work in the form of metallic lusters, which are a combination of pulverized precious metals and organic solvents. Commercially produced mother-of-pearl, gold, white gold, platinum, and silver lusters are all available.

Lusters can be applied by brush to the outside of a glazed and fired piece of ceramic work. Alternatively, some decals also utilize precious metals and can be applied as described here and on pages 107 and 108. Lusters can add an irresistible, mirrorlike gleam to your work. In the case of functional ware, however, be sure to warn customers that the pieces cannot go in the microwave, as the metal will spark.

As with both decals and china paints, it is important to clean your work with alcohol before applying luster. When you do apply the luster, a thin coat is best. (You can use

Artist Taylor Robenalt's Golden Eared Dog (above) and Two Swans with Roses (top) feature gold luster.

mineral spirits to thin the luster before painting, if necessary.) Using a dedicated brush, apply the luster in a well-ventilated area, as the fumes smell potent and are often toxic. One smooth coat should suffice. When you're finished, clean luster brushes with mineral spirits.

Note that luster painted over decals will cause the decal to burn out. If you are going to use both on your work, do two separate firings. Fire the decals first, then apply and fire the lusters.

Decals at Work with Julia Weber

Originally from Erie, Pennsylvania, Julia "Jewels" Weber spent time teaching pottery to Bhutanese refugees. Using clay as the basis for connecting cultures, Julia's class showcased how a young, motivated potter can make a difference in her community and address larger societal issues.

Julia has worked hard to establish a unique line of wheel-thrown and altered porcelain. Her process is remarkably complex, with great care and attention to detail paid at each step along the way. In this pitcher form (on page 111), for example, Julia began by throwing the body on the wheel. She then darted the foot and added a hand-built spout and handle. Afterward, she incised the lines in the foot and inlaid the carvings with a wash. She then bisque fired the pitcher to cone 04. She applied a coat of Odyssey White Gloss (page 174). She waxed select areas of the pitcher to control the second coat, her own gray glaze. She then fired the piece in oxidation to cone 6.

This is where the decals came in. She designed her mountain motif using Adobe Illustrator and created several different color schemes. She printed out the image with her color decal printer to create a china paint decal. She then applied the decal to the outside of the pitcher as described on pages 107 and 108, and fired it a third time to cone 014. Finally, she removed the pitcher from the kiln and sanded its foot level, and it took its place in the gallery.

Julia's work is a labor-intensive process, to be sure, and it takes the combination of glaze, form, and decoration all working together—not to mention three separate firings—to achieve this captivating result. The end product is a cohesive and balanced statement, a hard-edged, angular piece that remains inviting to use. It's a well-designed, modern update to the iconic and classic pitcher.

Stacking Mountain Mugs. Julia Claire Weber.
Photo courtesy of the artist.

The color schemes of decals created using a computer can be easily manipulated, resulting in a multitude of variations on a theme.

Stacking Mountain Mug. Julia Claire Weber.
Photo courtesy of the artist.

Incised lines, clear and gray glaze, and an original decal design make this a perfect container for a mountain lover's morning tea.

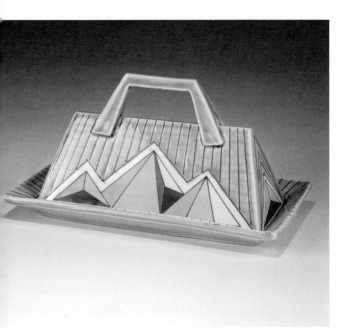

Mountain Butter Dish. Julia Claire Weber.
Photo courtesy of the artist.

The angular design of this butter dish works well with the geometric design of the mountain motif.

Darted Mountain Pitcher. Julia Claire Weber.
Photo courtesy of the artist.

This pitcher combines thrown and handbuilt elements, incised line decoration, tape resists, durable food-safe glazes, and decals, all working together to create a modern-looking piece with visual impact.

NON-GLAZE FINISHES

If you are making nonfunctional work, there are several ways to finish your bisque fired pieces without ever putting them in the kiln again. You can use acrylics, waxes, and spray paints to add additional color and sheen to your work. As always, make sure to apply these products in a well-ventilated area using proper protection, and according to the manufacturer's instructions. You could also use crayons, pencils, markers, and oil pastels on the surface of your work, then seal in the imagery using any of these spray-finishing products. You may want to do some testing before using these techniques in earnest, as these materials can change the color of the clay when they dry, sometimes giving it a slight orange sheen. (The best clear that I have found is the High Gloss Duncan Porcelain Enamel.)

Believe it or not, a sandblaster can be a useful tool to manipulate the surface of your piece. It takes down the sheen of a glaze and can even reveal the clay body beneath. Take proper safety precautions, such as wearing a dust mask or respirator, and make sure that you are using the right medium in your sandblaster. (I recommend alumina sand, as it contains no silica.) You can tape off areas or use vinyl decals to create sandblasted designs on your work as well.

Many possibilities exist for finishing your work with other materials besides traditional glaze. Epoxies, metal, and other mixed media additions are a possibility. Cloth, beads, gemstones, and even fur can all be used to enhance the surface of your work. Be open-minded and willing to experiment, and soon you may discover a new venue for your creative voice.

Molly Morning-glory uses a variety of non-glaze finishes in her work, such as sandblasting in these fanciful bird sculptures.

Alternative Finishes with Molly Morning-glory and Naim Cash

Molly and Naim work together with a variety of non-traditional materials, including spray paint, stickers, acrylic paint, and enamel.

A second-generation ceramic artist, Molly Morning-glory grew up around wheel-thrown pots of all sizes made by her parents, Maggie and Freeman Jones of Turtle Island Pottery. Although she can knock out a mean face mug in a matter of minutes, Molly's career has pushed away from the functional production work of her parents and toward large sculptures made in series, creatively decorated using a number of different techniques.

Naim Cash grew up writing graffiti and painting in Richmond, Virginia. He discovered ceramics in 2016, and it has been amazing to watch the progression of his work in three dimensions. The collaborative pieces between Molly and Naim are particularly captivating, relying on the technical skill of the two artists accompanied by a shared vision of creative intent.

In terms of process, the sculptures are hand-built from slabs, textured, and decorated with underglazes. The pieces are then bisque fired to cone 04. Any cracks or flaws are filled in with two-part moldable epoxy. Afterward, the work is taken outside, tape is applied, and Molly spray-paints isolated areas with gold for contrast and additional effects. Once she has completed her portion, Naim inherits the piece and applies acrylic paint in his own style, working from the decorations Molly has previously put in place. Once Naim has finished, the entire piece receives a coat of clear spray enamel to finish and seal it. Exciting, vibrant, and mysterious, this is the kind of work that is pushing the entire field of ceramic sculpture forward in America.

Head. Molly Morning-glory and Naim Cash.
Photos courtesy of Halima Flynt.

Tape and sticker resist, spray paints, and acrylics enliven the surface of this sculpture. The all-over decoration begs for the viewer to move around the piece, which can be appreciated from every angle.

RAKU AND ATMOSPHERIC FIRING

The term *atmospheric* refers to several types of firing in which gases and materials inside the kiln (and at times, post-firing) affect the surface of the work, changing the look, color, and texture of the clay and glaze. The most common forms of atmospheric firing are *raku*, wood, and salt or soda firing. Each of these styles of firing yields very different results, depending on your desired outcome.

The draw of atmospheric firing is easy to see: the surfaces are truly unique. There is also a magic in controlling some variables in decoration while leaving others to chance—an approach that appeals to some personality types more than others! There are a few downsides to these firing techniques, however. First, some firings, such as *raku*, leave clay porous. This means you cannot *raku* fire most functional work. Chance can also work against you; a bad firing may ruin many pots (although you can always refire).

The good news is that these firing types are most often communal. Since special kilns or tools are needed for all atmospheric firing, potters tend to fire work together. If your studio does not offer atmospheric firings, turn to the internet and see if any local studios have drop-in days or special workshops focused on these techniques. By firing with local experts, you have the best chance to find techniques, recipes, and firings that suit your local clay selection. You may make some new friends as well.

Raku firing is an accessible way to try atmospheric firing. Many communal studios offer *raku* classes and workshops.

CHAPTER 4

RAKU

Adapted from an ancient Japanese technique used during the tea ceremony, modern *raku* involves heating ceramic work to between 1,470 and 1,946 degrees Fahrenheit. Due to the low temperature and quick nature of the firing, the clay remains porous, and as such is ill suited for functional ware. Some potters will bisque fire work to be *raku* fired to cone 1, which allows the surface to still accept smoke, but provides a more durable finished product than with a cone 04 bisque. However, there are some glaze effects that can only be achieved in the *raku* kiln. The process of removing red-hot pots from the kiln and watching them ignite in a can of combustibles is certainly dynamic and exciting, but proper precautions must always be observed when firing *raku*, including always using tongs or appropriate gloves, keeping long hair tied back, and having a fire extinguisher on hand.

1. First, special low-fire glazes (see recipes on pages 186 to 189), often high in colorants such as copper carbonate, are applied to the surface of the work.

2. Once dry, the work is placed in a kiln with a removable top and fired quickly (in an hour or less) to the appropriate temperature. When the work reaches its peak temperature, the kiln is opened, and the glowing red work is removed with tongs. Ⓐ

3. The work is transferred to a can filled with combustibles, most often newspaper or sawdust or both. Ⓑ

4. The combustibles ignite, and the lid is closed on the container. This creates a heavily reducing, smoky atmosphere inside the container. Ⓒ Ⓓ

5. As a result, the porous clay body will become black. This type of firing allows the glazes to showcase some unique effects, including a beautiful type of crazing, and some remarkable metallic finishes, especially when copper is present in the glaze.

6. After cooling for 30 minutes in the can, the pots are removed and submerged in a bucket of water to "freeze" the colors. The pots can then be cleaned with an abrasive cleanser (such as Ajax) to get rid of any excess carbon and to brighten them up.

WOOD, SALT OR SODA, AND ASH

For millennia before the advent of electricity and use of fossil fuels, wood was the main source of fuel for kilns. Sourcing wood was an important part of any potter's daily operations. Potters in Germany began using wood from retired seafaring vessels and barrels that had been used to store salted herring. They noticed that the work fired with this wood often exhibited an orange flash. These potters theorized that the flash was caused by salt in the water that had impregnated the wood, so they intentionally began adding salt to their firings in order to increase the effect, and thus salt firing was born. Similar to wood ash landing on pots in a wood kiln, the salt or soda ash added to the kiln volatilizes (that is, turns from a solid into a gas), and the gas in the atmosphere spreads throughout the kiln, coating everything with a layer of sodium oxide, resulting in the "orange peel" texture on the work. Today, many potters salt and soda fire in gas kilns rather than wood firing, although many wood-fire potters also have a salt or soda chamber in their kiln.

When wood is used as the primary fuel source for firing ceramics, the ash created by the fire travels through the kiln, landing on the work inside. Wood ash contains calcium oxide and potassium oxide, as well as small amounts of sodium, zinc oxide, and other volatiles, all of which are common ingredients in many glazes. As such, the wood ash deposits form a layer of glaze on the surface of the work, which may be "naked," coated with slips, or glazed. The path of the flame across the work will greatly influence the look. For that reason, wood-fire potters take extra care when loading the kiln in order to consciously direct the flow of the flame over their pieces, hoping to create as much excitement as possible on the surface of the work.

Wood Firing with Josh Copus

I first met Josh Copus while he was finishing an undergraduate degree at the University of North Carolina in Asheville. This tall, charismatic, and boyishly good-looking potter immediately impressed me with his boundless enthusiasm for the craft, his passion for local materials (which he calls "wild clay"), and his commitment to creating community through firing.

Over the years, I have watched Josh dig 180,000 pounds of clay from a farmer's field in Leceister, North Carolina, establish a successful cooperative studio, the Clayspace Co-op, and build three large wood-fire kilns on his land in Madison County. In addition, Josh's fascination with the humble clay brick led him to start a successful mail-order brick company, an unlikely sounding but surprisingly successful endeavor. All the while, Josh has produced some of the most unique wood-fired forms: wheel-thrown and coiled pieces that are paddled, faceted, and slipped with the near maniacal energy of a man hell-bent on making a visual statement that represents his creative philosophy.

If you are drawn to the finishes of Josh's pots or those of other wood-fire potters, perhaps it is a firing method you should investigate. Following are some of Josh's thoughts and wisdom, should you have the chance to add work to a wood-fire kiln near you, or at a workshop.

Wedge. Josh Copus. *Photo courtesy of the artist.*

Finger wipes through slip create action and movement on this stately piece.

"Wood firing is many things, but boring is not amongst them. The process itself is never dull. My advice if you're just getting started with wood firing is to work hard and listen harder. Volunteer to do the overnight shift. Fire as many different kilns as you can and learn from as many different people as possible. But most importantly: *learn what you like, figure out what you want to say, and make it yours.*

"Personally, I want things to feel like rocks, like they were in a shipwreck, or like someone dug them up out of the ground. Wood firing is the best option for me to achieve this. I'm not beholden to it, though . . . if it didn't produce the effects I was interested in, I would finish my work another way and just have a bonfire with friends. It's a lot easier.

"Now I can tell you the basics of firing a kiln in five minutes, but you can still spend the rest of your life trying to figure it out. My best advice is to learn the temperature and atmosphere zones that the kiln you're using creates naturally. Accentuate those zones instead of trying to make a kiln fire 'even' . . . you can use them to your advantage to create a variety of different effects. You'll find clays and glazes will change completely in different areas of the kiln. If you know what you're doing, you can make one glaze do ten different things in the same firing.

"I've found the notion that there are good and bad spots in a kiln to be completely untrue. There are only the right spots for the right pots. I can't even count how many times I've heard someone say 'I don't like the back' or 'the front is the best spot' when we are loading. Over the years, I've seen plenty of bad work come out of the front face of a wood kiln. It doesn't really matter how good the surface of a pot is if the lid is fused to the jar by heavy ash deposits.

"Wood firing can take you to places you never dreamed of, but it can also bring you to your knees. Remember that the sun will always come up again tomorrow. If you keep showing up, you'll figure it out."

Large Stone Vessel. Josh Copus. *Photo courtesy of the artist.*

No glaze was applied to this piece. All of the color is a result of the wood ash and path of the flame over the pot, and its reaction to the sphere of slip applied on the faceted sidewall.

Iron Stone Vessel. Josh. Copus. *Photo courtesy of the artist.*

Atmospheric glazing allows the artist to show off the beauty of the clay itself. Large particles of rock are visible in the surface of this piece, made from hand-dug "wild clay."

Moon Jar. Josh Copus. *Photo courtesy of the artist.*

Seashells used to support the piece leave a beautiful recollection of its firing. The seashells kept the piece from fusing to the kiln shelf, as an alternative to wadding. The jar was fired on its side, which affects the movement of the atmospheric glaze over the form.

Linda McFarling and Salt Firing

I have always been inspired by this simple, direct goal of salt-fire potter Linda McFarling: "My aim as a functional potter is to make pots that honor the rich traditions of the past, while hopefully adding to them." Greatly influenced by Japanese and Korean pots, Linda has, over the course of her career, successfully updated classic forms, putting her own personal stamp on tradition, and in the process has created some truly dynamic and innovative salt-fired forms.

As she constantly searches for new avenues of expression, in recent years she has expanded her repertoire from wheel-thrown pots to include a series of beautifully extruded vases. Linda is one of those rare artists who is also a brilliant teacher, and her classes are a hot ticket. Her students are attracted not just to the austere beauty of the work she creates, but to the energy and enthusiasm she brings to her teaching. Salt- and soda-firing guru Linda McFarling is a living national treasure, in my opinion.

If you are soon embarking on a journey into learning salt firing, here is some advice from Linda, gathered from years of teaching:

Tripod Jar. Linda McFarling. *Photo courtesy of the artist.*
The salt and soda in the atmosphere provide all the color and texture on the surface of this covered jar.

1. Remember to wad everything! Wadding is material that the work will sit on in the kiln, preventing it from fusing to the kiln shelf in an atmospheric firing (recipe for wadding on page 193).

2. Make sure you have enough kosher salt and soda ash on hand. About 3 to 5 pounds of each should be sufficient for a 20-cubic-foot kiln. These materials can be placed in newspaper "burritos" and thrown inside the kiln, or mixed with water and put in a commercial sprayer.

3. Make sure your equipment, including burners, blowers, and sprayers, are in working order.

4. Make sure glazes are not too thick and glazes that run are not on the fire face.

5. Never use a rubber wand for spraying! It will melt in the flame and leave you scrambling for a way to introduce your salt or soda ash into the kiln.

6. It matters how you load. Know your slips and take your time. Your firing and pots depend on it.

7. I would advise anyone interested in pursuing salt and soda to work with an experienced professional. Find work you love and study with its creator if at all possible. There are many little nuances that will have such an impact on your success or failure. Your learning curve will be much shorter!

Yunomis. Linda McFarling. *Photo courtesy of the artist.*
The combination of glaze applied before firing and atmospheric glaze from the kiln give these yunomis a special, tactile appeal.

Oven Casserole. Linda McFarling. *Photo courtesy of the artist.*

Glazed and unglazed areas of this casserole work in conjunction to form an aesthetically pleasing finished product.

Olive Oil Ewer. Linda McFarling. *Photo courtesy of the artist.*

A single coat of glaze breaks over the raised areas, highlighting the textured surface of this ewer.

Teapot. Linda McFarling. *Photo courtesy of the artist.*

Heavy salt deposits decorate the body of this teapot, while the color and texture of the cane handle complete the visual statement.

Olive Oil Ewer.
Linda McFarling.
Photo courtesy of the artist.

Salt and soda in the atmosphere of the kiln will affect the way your glazes perform.

GALLERY

Crystalline Vase. Frank Vickery. *Photo courtesy of Dick Dickinson Studios.*

Stunning blue crystals accentuate a wheel-thrown bottle form.

Golden Eared Bunny and Dog. Taylor Robenalt.
Photo courtesy of the artist.

Underglazes and lusters contrast with the stark black underglaze and white porcelain.

The Other One Crystalline Vase. Bruce Gholson.
Photo courtesy of the artist.

Detail shot of crystals meeting to form a lovely pattern on the surface of this pot.

Crystalline Orb. Frank Vickery. *Photo courtesy of Dick Dickinson Studios.*

The glaze transitions nicely from the near pure white at the top of the piece to the large crystals floating in the amber colored background at the base.

Crystalline Matt Vase. Samantha Henneke.
Photo courtesy of the artist.

The runny glaze at the neck provides downward movement on this piece, in contrast to the bubbly effect of the crystals in a matte background.

Molybdenum Crystalline Vase. Bruce Gholson.
Photo courtesy of the artist.

Radical rainbow crystals are the result of the use of molybdenum in the glaze.

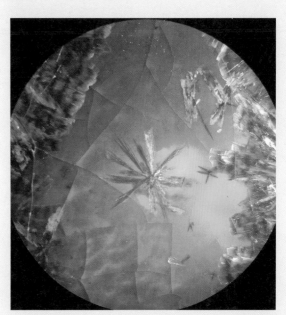

Crystalline Glaze Under a Microscope. Evan Cornish-Keefe.
Photo courtesy of the artist.

A microscope allows a detailed look at crystal growth in a glaze.

Oval Platter. Bill Campbell. *Photo courtesy of the artist.*

Gigantic crystals cover the interior of this platter. This is a result of skillful application and careful firing.

Bent Nova Bowl.
Bill Campbell.
Photo courtesy of the artist.

The fluid glaze pools up in the incised lines of this pleasantly altered bowl, which also features some iridescent effects and beautiful crystal growth.

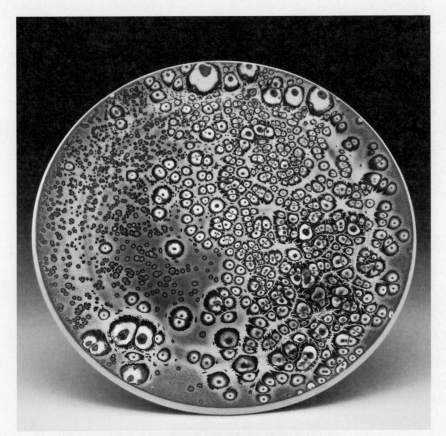

White Plate.
Adrian Sandstrom. *Photo courtesy of the artist.*

Neutral tones of gray, black, and white dance together on the surface of this platter, suggesting microbiotic life under a microscope.

Crystalline Bowl.
Evan Cornish Keefe. *Photo courtesy of the artist.*

The spectacular crystal growth on the rim of this bowl contrasts nicely with the speckled clay peeking through the glaze on its interior.

5

FIRING, FINISHING, AND FIXING

About thirty thousand years ago, humans began making and firing figurines in fire pits. With experience, these early ceramic artists were able to increase the temperature of their fires, eventually constructing the first primitive kilns within small caves by digging into the mountainside. Around seven thousand years ago, Egyptians discovered a clay body amenable to firing composed predominantly of glass and fluxes. The advent of Egyptian paste represents the beginning of glaze history, as potters began to experiment with the use of these materials on top of clay vessels to create a skin—a less permeable surface on the pot.

Fast-forward to the modern era, and you'll find ceramic material scientists able to use their knowledge of the periodic table to create working maps of ceramic materials and their interactions. The performance of these materials is predictable, but it relies on skillful firing, which is what we'll investigate in this chapter. If great attention is paid to the making and glazing of the work, but the firing is done casually or without care, the result can be disappointing. However, if the same careful attention to detail in the making and glazing is paid to the firing the work, the results can be not only spectacular but replicable as well.

THE BASICS OF FIRING

Over the past several thousand years, humans have used many different materials to fuel their kilns, including animal waste, wood, straw, and in modern times, coal, oil, natural gas, propane, and even reclaimed methane from landfills. Yet the majority of kilns in the United States, United Kingdom, and continental Europe now rely on electricity or natural gas. It is worth noting, however, that the electricity you use can still come from a less-than-desirable source, such as coal. When you imagine a piece of coal burning in order to heat up the elements in an electric kiln, you will find new inspiration for efficiency.

In this chapter, we will focus on the two types of kilns that are most widely used (electric and gas), suggest firing schedules that are appropriate for different types of work, and discuss ways to correct physical defects in the glazing process. But first, let's look at the initial firing of work, the bisque firing.

BISQUE FIRING

Most potters bisque fire their work before glazing, heating the pots to between 1,728 and 1,946 degrees Fahrenheit so that they become less fragile than greenware, but are still porous enough to accept glaze in its liquid form. When you are bisque firing, there are several important considerations.

For all firings, you'll want to make sure that your kiln is located in a well-ventilated area or has had a commercial vent installed, as some offgassing of materials will occur during the firing. Make sure that the work is bone dry before loading it into the kiln. (You can use the kiln to force-dry pieces, but it creates extra wear and tear on the kiln elements, and can use more fossil fuels.) You want to fit as many pots as possible into the kiln to a certain extent. However, you should avoid excessive stacking or nesting. This can affect the ability of organic and inorganic material to burn out of the ware, which can affect your glazes in subsequent firings (see pages 134 and 146).

During the bisque firing process, several changes happen in the clay. First, non-chemically bonded water (H_2O that lies between molecules of other material and has no electrostatic attraction to them) will evaporate up to the boiling point of water, usually around 212 degrees Fahrenheit. Many potters will hold the temperature at 180 degrees Fahrenheit for between thirty minutes and six hours to make sure that all this water has left the clay. This process is called candling, and it can be tested by holding a piece of glass up to an open spyhole in the kiln. If condensation develops on the glass, there is more water to be evaporated out of the clay. You should wait until the glass no longer fogs up before turning up the kiln. If this water, referred to as the "physical water," remains when the temperature is raised above the boiling point of water, this water will expand as it turns to steam and can cause the work to crack—or even blow up into a million tiny pieces. It is crucial to make sure that the work has fully dried before continuing the firing.

Note: *When you're loading a bisque kiln (in fact, when loading any kiln), be sure to line up the kiln posts directly underneath one another so they form a column that runs up the kiln. Staggered kiln furniture can result in warped kiln shelves, or worse, can create so much tension in the shelves that they crack, and (woe unto the unwary) the whole stack implodes.*

Electric kilns are the most common method of firing in studios today.

Between 572 and 1,292 degrees Fahrenheit, organic material in the clay begins to burn out. Between 842 and 1,112 degrees Fahrenheit, the chemically bonded water (water that has an electrostatic attraction to other molecules in the clay) is released. At 1,063 degrees Fahrenheit, the quartz in the clay will go through a process called quartz inversion, which involves a linear expansion of the material. Some potters slow the rate of climb to 100 degrees an hour through this process, while others continue at the same rate of climb. Inorganic materials, including carbon and sulfur, begin to burn out at 1,292 degrees Fahrenheit and are released as carbon dioxide and sulfur dioxide. Above 1,450 degrees Fahrenheit, frits, soda ash, and boron begin to melt, and the clay sinters (becomes denser as the molecules realign in more of a lattice structure).

Most potters bisque fire to somewhere between cone 08 (1,728 degrees Fahrenheit) and cone 04 (1,946 degrees Fahrenheit). I recommend firing to the higher of the two temperatures so that the heat fully penetrates thicker areas and allows all the organic and inorganic materials to burn out. Also, a lower firing will result in more porous bisque that will absorb glaze quicker. If you bisque fire to a different temperature, you will need to adjust the length of time you submerge your pot in glaze.

Whether you are bisque firing in an electric kiln or a gas kiln, an oxidizing atmosphere should be maintained. If there isn't enough oxygen to burn the carbon and sulfur at this stage of the firing, they will burn out during glaze firing, causing pinholes.

If your electric kiln is programmable using a controller, we recommend using a slow cone fire program to bisque, rather than a medium or fast program.

Standard (slow) bisque fire profile:

Segment 1	80 degrees per hour to 250 degrees Fahrenheit
Segment 2	200 degrees per hour to 1,000 degrees Fahrenheit
Segment 3	100 degrees per hour to 1,100 degrees Fahrenheit
Segment 4	180 degrees per hour to 1,500 degrees Fahrenheit
Segment 5	108 degrees per hour to 1,946 degrees Fahrenheit

This firing schedule will take approximately twelve hours and is recommended for the majority of bisque fired ceramic work. For large, thick, or sculptural work, we use a slightly different program.

Celadon Stein. Gabriel Kline. Careful attention paid to the firing will result in a beautiful, replicable finish, as seen in this stein by the author. *Photo courtesy of Steve Mann.*

Large or thick bisque fire profile:

Segment 1	75 degrees per hour to 180 degrees Fahrenheit (Hold at this temperature for two to eight hours, depending on the size or thickness of the piece.)
Segment 2	150 degrees per hour to 900 degrees Fahrenheit
Segment 3	75 degrees per hour to 1,200 degrees Fahrenheit
Segment 4	175 degrees per hour to 1,946 degrees Fahrenheit

For kilns that do not have a programmable controller, you will have to manually turn up the kiln at several intervals. Start by keeping the kiln settings on low for three hours, or until no moisture appears on a piece of glass placed in front of a spyhole. If the kiln is vented with a fan, be sure to turn it off when you do this test in order to assess accurately the moisture level in the clay. Turn the kiln on medium for three hours, and then move the kiln up to high until it reaches temperature, determined by the witness cones in the kiln.

For most bisque firing in a manual electric kiln:

Segment 1	all three sections of the kiln on low for three hours
Segment 2	all three sections of the kiln on medium for three hours
Segment 3	all three sections of the kiln on high until it reaches temperature

For large or sculptural work in a manual electric kiln:

Segment 1	Turn the bottom elements on low for two hours.
Segment 2	Turn the middle elements on low for two hours.
Segment 3	Turn the top elements on low for two hours.
Segment 4	Turn the bottom elements on medium for two hours.
Segment 5	Turn the middle elements on medium for two hours.
Segment 6	Turn the middle elements on high for two hours.
Segment 7	Turn the bottom elements on high for two hours.
Segment 8	Turn the middle elements on high for two hours.
Segment 9	Turn the top elements on high until the kiln reaches temperature.

GLAZE FIRING

Once you're familiar with bisque firing, glaze firing will not seem difficult. However, there are certainly key differences in firing schedules and in loading the kiln. In terms of loading, it is important that each piece be at least ¼ inch away from any other pieces of work in the kiln and from any kiln posts. As mentioned on pages 46 and 48, no piece should have glaze on the bottom or within ¼ inch of the bottom of the piece to allow for some movement of the glaze in the firing. Unlike in bisque firing, you should not nest pieces inside each other during glaze firing. Contact could result in pieces fusing together as the molten glaze cools.

The kiln shelves should be kiln-washed on the tops, leaving a ¼-inch border around the edge to avoid any kiln wash flaking off and landing on the shelves or work below. (Kiln wash is a blend

Gas kilns, such as the Geil kiln pictured, are used for reduction firing (see pages 141 to 144).

of refractory materials mixed with water that will resist glaze that has run off a piece. See recipe on page 193.) Additionally, any experimental pieces, or pieces that would exhibit runny glaze, should be cookied. A cookie is a fired, kiln-washed disk of clay that is placed underneath the work during firing. The cookie prevents any runny glaze from landing on the kiln shelves, which can be very expensive to replace. (See page 138 for more on cookies.)

Similar to bisque firing, during glaze firing the kiln posts should be aligned, not staggered, in order to create the strongest stack possible and put the least amount of pressure on the kiln shelves. Kiln shelves are susceptible to cracking under uneven pressure.

You will find many different ways of addressing runny or "risky" glazes in different studios.

In our opinion, the hierarchy of practices is as follows:

- **Good:** Make sure your shelves are kiln-washed on the top only, ¼ inch in from the edges.

- **Better:** Place work on kiln-washed cookies on kiln-washed shelves.

- **Best:** Place work on wadding on kiln-washed cookies on kiln-washed shelves.

Raku is an exciting firing process that provides finished results faster than any other method of firing, though the work becomes ornamental only, and should not be used for food or drink.

Tisha Cook's Superlative Kiln Cookies

As the kiln tech for the large, front-loading Geil downdraft kiln at Odyssey, Tisha Cook has established several exemplary studio practices that have become teaching tools for all of our students. A terrific potter and a former cake decorator, Tisha Cook's attention to detail is unparalleled in the studio. (She first throws very exacting forms, then adds facets, carvings, and elegant feet, handles, and knobs while each piece is leather hard.) Her skillfully dipped, poured, and sprayed glazes interact in the kiln to produce dazzling combinations, often forming eutectics resulting in rivulets of ash and crystal highlighted against a satiny base. Post firing, Tisha adds even more detail to the pieces, inlaying handmade paper and custom reed handles. She even dyes the reeds herself to match the color scheme of the glaze and paper!

Due to her use of these risky glazes, Tisha has developed a system for firing her work that minimizes loss. Her practice uses balls of wadding on top of a kiln-washed cookie, which is then placed on top of a kiln-washed kiln shelf. While this may seem labor-intensive, she saves herself an enormous amount of work when unloading the kiln and when grinding the bottoms of the pots for smoothness. Because her pieces have already been treated with care and presence in their making, forming, bisque firing, and glazing, her system gives the pots the dignity and respect they deserve. Tisha loses very few pieces and saves countless more through this technique. I have always appreciated, too, that the cookies themselves are aesthetically pleasing, having been made from clay rolled to ⅛ inch thick, cleanly cut with a custom die, the edges cleaned, and neatly kiln-washed.

When you are making your own cookies, it's a good idea to make sure your cookies are made from a cone 10 clay body, even if you are firing to a lower cone. If a cookie is made from a low-fire clay and is accidentally placed in a high-fire kiln, you will produce a melted puddle of clay that has permanently fused itself to your kiln shelf. You should also avoid using cookies that are warped or have already had glaze run onto them. Use a cookie underneath any experimental glazes you might be trying for the first time, or any combinations that you know to be risky or runny. Be consistent with this practice and over time you will spare yourself many headaches. Cookies save lots of pots, shatters in platters, and holes in bowls!

Making and using kiln cookies like this one may seem unnecessarily labor-intensive, but you will end up saving yourself considerable effort—and probably some pots, cups, and bowls, too!

Celadon Covered Bowl with Reed Handle and Inlaid Paper. Tisha Cook. *Photo courtesy of Steve Mann.*

Subtleties, such as the crosshatching beneath the knob on the lid of this covered jar, give the viewer a variety of enjoyable details to appreciate.

Perfume Bottles with Stoppers. Tisha Cook.
Photo courtesy of Steve Mann.

Carefully sprayed glazes create movement horizontally through these stoppered bottles. A glaze-catching foot with a stable glaze prevents the flowing glaze above it from running off the pots.

Cobalt Covered Bowl with Reed Handle and Inlaid Paper. Tisha Cook.
Photo courtesy of Steve Mann.

A semi-translucent cobalt glaze highlights the stamped decoration and carved decoration on the body of this pot. All the details work together to create a refined look. Tisha Cook dyes the cane reed for her handles to match the inlaid paper decoration, applied after glaze firing.

In terms of the glaze firing schedule, the rate of climb will be higher than that of bisque firing for the first part of the firing, as the clay no longer needs to shed water or burn out organic materials. However, the rate of climb will be slowed toward the top of the firing in order to give the glaze materials time to mature. Glazes will often release gases and bubble before fluxing out to coat the piece in a smooth liquid layer of glaze. Going slower at the top of a glaze firing allows time for these processes to take place. If you rush the top of the firing, you may find bubbles in your glaze or bare spots on your ware. As the kiln begins to cool, the liquid glaze will "freeze" back into a solid on the surface of your piece. Glazed work should be allowed to cool to room temperature before unloading.

Standard (medium) glaze fire profile:

Segment 1	200 degrees per hour to 250 degrees Fahrenheit
Segment 2	400 degrees per hour to 1,000 degrees Fahrenheit
Segment 3	180 degrees per hour to 1,150 degrees Fahrenheit
Segment 4	300 degrees per hour to 1,694 degrees Fahrenheit
Segment 5	120 degrees per hour until the kiln reaches temperature

Another program you can use, developed by Pete Pinnell, is a down fire program to cone 6, in which the kiln continues to fire after it has reached temperature, causing a slower cooling process. This program encourages crystal growth and can combat glaze defects such as pinholing, which will be discussed in detail later in this chapter.

Down fire profile:

Segment 1	100 degrees per hour to 200 degrees Fahrenheit
Segment 2	450 degrees per hour to 1,900 degrees Fahrenheit
Segment 3	108 degrees per hour to 2,196 degrees Fahrenheit
Segment 4	150 degrees per hour to 1,700 degrees Fahrenheit

Note: The Skutt cone table suggests 2,232 degrees Fahrenheit for a rate of climb of 108 degrees an hour to reach cone 6. However, due to the down fire and the additional heat work that occurs during it, I have found that firing to the lower top temperature of 2,196 degrees Fahrenheit yields a great cone 6 firing, while firing to 2,232 degrees Fahrenheit sometimes results in an overfired kiln. Also, if you are using a manual kiln, you can down fire by turning the elements back to medium after the kiln reaches temperature for two to three hours.

Glaze myth #412: The computer (or kiln sitter) will always give you a perfect reading.

While the technology is convenient, both kiln sitters and computers can be unreliable at shutting off the kiln at the appropriate time. The kiln sitter can fail, relays can stick, or the controller and thermocouple can become miscalibrated. These problems will cause the kiln to either shut off before it has reached temperature (underfire) or continue to fire after the kiln has reached temperature (overfire). In order to avoid those problems, we highly encourage the use of witness cones in the kiln. Witness cones are placed in the kiln in front of the spyholes so that they can be seen during the firing. You should make sure to be around your kiln at the top of the firing so that, if the kiln shuts off early before the witness cones have melted, you can turn the kiln back on until the witness cones have melted, and then turn the kiln off manually. Similarly, if the kiln reaches temperature but continues to fire, you can turn the kiln off manually in order to avoid severely overfiring the work.

REDUCTION FIRING

For reduction firing in a gas kiln, you will need to monitor both the rate of climb and the atmosphere inside the kiln. During the periods of reduction, the carbon monoxide in the kiln will seek out the oxygen molecules in the clay and glaze (most easily released by iron oxide and copper oxide) in order to continue burning. The reduced number of oxygen molecules in the clay and glaze will affect the color of both. For example, copper that would look green or blue in oxidation may turn oxblood red in reduction.

Reduction firing creates unique results, altering both glazes and clay bodies in a different way than oxidation. This set from Cayce Kolstad features Roger's Green and Yellow Salt glaze on a buff stoneware clay body.

The firing should begin with oxidation up to cone 012 (1,582 degrees Fahrenheit). When the kiln hits that temperature, push in the damper to deprive the kiln of oxygen. You want to achieve a "climbing reduction," in which the temperature inside the kiln goes up approximately 60 degrees per hour, or 1 degree per minute, up to cone 04 (1,946 degrees Fahrenheit). If the temperature begins to fall when you push in the damper, gently pull it back out until you achieve this rate of climb. You may see a yellow flame with an orange tip coming out of the chimney and spyholes, indicating a reducing atmosphere. After this initial reduction, the damper can be pulled back out and an oxidizing flame, indicated by a bluish color, can be used until it reaches 200 degrees below the top temperature. At this point, you want to push in the damper a second time to reduce the surface of the glazes further.

In order to measure the degree of reduction, you can use an oxiprobe to measure the amount of oxygen inside the kiln. However, these are quite expensive and easily broken. Alternatively, and for no money, you can look at the color of the flame. As mentioned above, a reducing kiln will have a yellow to orange flame coming out of the chimney and spyholes. An oxidizing flame is a bluish color. As the degree of reduction can greatly affect the colors you can achieve, you will want to experiment with the damper settings, taking detailed notes as you fire.

Reduction glaze fire profile (for cone 10):

Segment 1	Leaving damper open, climb 100 degrees per hour to 200 degrees Fahrenheit.
Segment 2	Leaving damper open, climb 400 degrees per hour to 1,582 degrees Fahrenheit.
Segment 3	Push damper in until rate of climb is 60 degrees per hour to 1,946 degrees Fahrenheit.
Segment 4	Pull damper out until rate of climb is 100 degrees per hour to 2,150 degrees Fahrenheit.
Segment 5	Push damper in until a yellow-orange flame is coming out of the chimney and spyholes, indicating a reducing atmosphere, and climb 60 to 100 degrees per hour until the kiln reaches temperature according to the witness cones (approximately 2,350 degrees Fahrenheit).

Note: This profile is for a Geil downdraft kiln. Not all gas-fired kilns will require adjusting the damper as described in segment 5.

It's optional, but some people like to oxidize at the top of the firing for half an hour with the goal of brightening the colors. In order to oxidize, pull out the damper to let sufficient air into the kiln. Experiment with this technique to see if it works for you and your glazes.

Whether your glaze firing is oxidizing in an electric kiln or reducing in a gas kiln, once the firing is complete, the kiln should be allowed to

Notice how Spearmint (page 178) looks on the same clay body when fired to cone 5 (left) and cone 7 (right).

cool slowly. Only open the kiln once it's back to room temperature. If you have to peek—and do try to resist the impulse—make sure the kiln is 240 degrees Fahrenheit or cooler, and do not open the kiln door until the temperature is 150 degrees Fahrenheit or cooler.

CONSIDER FIRING RANGE

Glaze myth #218: *Cones 05, 6, and 10 are the only cones used for glazing.*

Ceramic materials all have a firing range in which they become increasingly fluid as they reach their melting point. With the right combination of materials, possibilities for dynamic results are available at nearly any cone. Commercially produced glazes are generally formulated to mature at their cone 05, 6, or 10

standards. There are, however, notable exceptions. For example, Amaco low-fire reds, which look best at cone 06, often burn out when fired higher. While glazes may be formulated or adjusted to mature at a specific point, many (but not all of these) will display attractive qualities across a spectrum of temperatures and atmospheres.

At first blush, it may seem inadvisable to fire your work to a higher cone than the recipe suggests. It is important to note that firing this way is different than overfiring. The very term *overfire* suggests that you have overdone it, gone overboard, reached too far. The terrible images of pots stuck to kiln shelves, pools of glaze overflowing onto other pots below, and of donning the dust mask and safety glasses to use the angle grinder come to mind. Yet experience has taught me that if done in a controlled manner and with proper precautions, firing higher than the recommended cone can reveal dynamic results. In my experience, some cone 6 glazes can look more mature at cone 7. There are several glazes that can be pushed further than that, and still look appealing at cone 8 or even cone 10.

I encourage you to look at the process as reaching the top of the material's firing range. When you are intentionally firing your glazes this way, you will first want to make sure that the clay body you are using can handle the firing range. Many cone 6 clay bodies are even more vitrified (becoming more glasslike, and able to absorb less water) at cone 7 and sound a beautiful ring when struck. Similarly, many cone 10 clays intended for food or drink begin to vitrify sufficiently at cone 7. When you intend to intentionally "fire hot," it is important to make sure that the clay body being used can handle the heat being applied and is sufficiently mature to withstand the rigors of its intended use. Do make sure that you test your clay body first, as some cone 6 bodies may bloat or warp, and some cone 10 clays may not vitrify sufficiently for long-term use. In order to avoid unnecessary loss, and before you begin to utilize this strategy in earnest, make sure you test, test, test!

Some examples of cone 6 glazes that can be successfully fired to cone 7 include Spearmint, Chun Celadon, and Chameleon Gray-Green; recipes and suggested ranges are found starting on page 170.

Likewise, you can intentionally fire a glaze to a lower temperature than the recipe suggests. For example, a glossy glaze fired at cone 10 may make a fantastic semimatte at cone 6. Experiment with the cone 10 glazes in your studio. Do be cautious if the work is going to be used with food or drink. Often the results look great but may not be suitable for functional work. If you are going to intentionally "fire cool" for functional work, make sure to test your results once they come out using the scratch test for durability, the lemon test to check leaching, and the microwave and freezer tests to ensure the work can handle thermal shock. (These tests are described in detail beginning on page 150.)

Van Guilder Blue Ash is a great glaze that performs well at cone 6 to cone 10. If it is runny at 6, be aware that it is runnier at 10, so use with caution and keep at the very top of the pot. Always use cookies. (See recipe on page 193.) Two remarkable materials to note with incredible firing ranges are Amaco LG 10, which makes a great clear glaze from cone 05 all the way to cone 10, and Fish Sauce Slip (recipe on page 191), with a similar extended firing range from cone 04 to cone 10.

Cobalt Platter. Gabriel Kline. *Photo courtesy of Steve Mann.*

Precise application of layered glazes and careful attention to firing can give you tremendous results.

CLEANING IT UP

At this point, you should be unloading a flawless kiln of remarkably dynamic pots. Even so, there will probably be a few things to clean up from time to time.

For those pieces that do have glaze run off the side, the sacred art of grinding should be employed to clean the base of the pot. This will remove any excess glaze, thus returning it to a level and smooth finish. First use a Dremel with a rotary diamond bit to separate the pot from the cookie. Next, use a Dremel or bench grinder to remove excess glaze. Or better yet, make a custom diamond sanding bat. Diamond sanding disks are available commercially at most glass blowing supply stores and may be glued onto a throwing bat. When placed on the potter's wheel, it will transform the equipment into a proper grinding station. You can then wet sand the piece by periodically wetting the disk with water. This will alleviate most of the dust, but you should always wear a dust mask or respirator and safety goggles when grinding.

A diamond sanding disk makes quick work of any excess glaze on the bottom of a pot.

A Dremel tool with a rotary diamond bit is a useful tool for removing small debris.

I recommend using a 100-grit diamond bat initially and finer grades of sandpaper or diamond sanding sponges after that. The diamond bat also does a great job of leveling pieces that may have warped slightly in the kiln. (Goodbye to that unfortunate and obnoxious wobble we have all experienced while sitting at uneven café tables.)

If the surface of your work is disagreeable coming out of the kiln, all is not lost. You can still reglaze and/or refire. The challenge in refiring glazed work is to get fresh glaze to stick to the glazed surface. Some people heat the pot up in the kiln to about 150 degrees Fahrenheit and then reglaze. The warm surface of the pot causes the water in the glaze to evaporate almost immediately and helps the glaze adhere to the piece more quickly.

Another—and in my opinion better—method is to use an additive called ATP enhancer, available at most pottery supply stores. Add just three to four drops of the enhancer per ounce of glaze. Once stirred, the glaze thickens to a near-foamy consistency, and it will stick to the surface of the pot without running. (You do not have to heat the pot at all with this method.)

Refiring improves the quality of a substandard piece about half of the time, but sometimes the piece looks worse after refiring. If it was a piece that would have ended up in the dumpster without refiring, it certainly can't hurt to try, and sometimes you will transform a mediocre piece, *mirabile dictu*, into one that truly sings! Just keep in mind that there's a risk inherent in refiring.

COMMON PROBLEMS

Even for the most seasoned pro, things may go awry. Even porcelain factories, which have refined the production process to a science, have massive shard piles of unsuccessful pieces out back. For the clay artist, there's not much worse than opening a kiln and finding pieces with problems such as pinholing, dunting, crawling, crazing, or shivering. Luckily the most common problems have common causes as well.

Pinholing Ⓐ Pinholes are tiny bubbles in the glaze that freeze as the glaze cools. In addition to being unattractive, they can also be dangerous, as they break easily and can be very sharp. Pinholes are generally caused by organic or inorganic material burning out during glaze firing. In order to overcome pinholing, make sure to bisque fire your work to cone 04 in order to burn out as much organic and inorganic material as possible. If the problem persists, try adding more flux to the glaze recipe.

(A)

Dunting: Dunts are cracks that go through both the glaze and the clay body, ruining the structural integrity of a piece. If a piece dunts, it is almost surely lost. Dunting is commonly due to cooling work too fast through quartz inversion. To alleviate dunting, first make sure that you are cooling the kiln slowly, particularly through quartz inversion (1,063 degrees Fahrenheit) and at around 450 degrees Fahrenheit, where the last bit of contraction of the ceramic materials will occur.

Crawling Ⓑ Crawling refers to glaze that separates into clumps during firing, forming beads on the surface of a piece. Crawling is often due to glaze that is too thick (cracking in the dry state is an indicator) or glazed work that has not had sufficient time to dry before firing. In order to alleviate crawling, make sure that you have tested your glazes to find their ideal specific gravity and count. If the glaze cracks before it is put in the kiln, we recommend washing the glaze off, allowing the piece to dry for twenty-four hours, and then reglazing. Similarly, it is best to allow glazed work to dry overnight before loading it into a kiln to ensure that all of the water contained in the glaze has evaporated before heat is applied. It should be noted that sometimes crawling can look very nice, and that there are several glazes that are formulated to crawl, including Cassie's Bling (see recipe on page 181).

Ⓑ

Crazing © Crazing refers to a network of cracks that appear in the surface of the glaze after firing. "Delayed crazing" may continue to for weeks or even months after the piece has been removed from the kiln. Crazing is due to a difference in expansion and contraction rates between the clay body and the glaze, which puts the glaze under tension. (The glaze shrinks more than the clay.) The cracks appear to relieve this tension, much as an earthquake alleviates the tension of tectonic plates. In order to overcome crazing, try reducing high-expansion fluxes such as soda or adding silica to the glaze recipe to alter its coefficient of expansion.

Shivering: The opposite of crazing, shivering is a dangerous condition in which the glaze flakes off the clay body, often in very sharp splinters. When the clay body contracts considerably more than the glaze, the glaze is put under compression, causing it to flake off the piece. You can try adding 5 to 10 percent soda feldspar, nepheline syenite, or Ferro Frit 3110 to normalize the expansion rates between the clay and glaze. Alternatively, you could substitute high-expansion oxides like spodumene or lithium carbonate.

TESTING DURABILITY

If you are a maker of functional ware to be used with food or drink, it is important to test the durability of your product. While there are laboratories that will perform a battery of durability tests for a fee, there are several tests you can perform at your home or in your studio that will indicate whether your work is appropriate for functional ware. Once you are satisfied with the visual look of your piece coming out of the kiln, subject the work to the following tests to ensure that it will perform admirably in a number of different scenarios.

Some glazes may give an indication of their suitability for functional work simply by their recipes. Glazes with high amounts of colorants (such as those with more than 4 percent copper carbonate), and glazes with low silica and low alumina immediately suggest that they be used only on work that will not be used with food or drink. Some toxic materials may leach out of the glaze in the presence of acids such as vinegar or coffee. If you are in doubt about a certain glaze, first use the tests below. If these tests are inconclusive, or if the glaze seems at all questionable, send a piece off to the lab.

Freezer test: Place the piece in your freezer overnight. The next morning, preheat your oven to 350 degrees Fahrenheit and heat the piece, moving it directly from freezer to oven, for a half hour. Clay and glaze used for functional work should be able to handle this stress. If the piece cracks or crazes when making the transition from cold to hot, you may want to consider using a different clay or a different set of glazes for your work. If the piece passes the test, you can be assured that the future owner can use it without much worry.

Scratch test: Take a key from your key ring and draw it back and forth over a small area of the glazed surface of your piece. If the key leaves a score mark that cannot be removed with a gentle buffing by your finger, silverware would score the surface similarly and will leave a darkened surface over time. While this scoring is not necessarily a problem in terms of function, and can be removed with products such as Bar Keepers Friend, you may want to adjust your recipes to include more silica and/or flux, providing a glossier surface.

Lemon test: Squeeze the juice of a lemon onto a horizontal glazed surface of your piece. Place the rest of the lemon in the juice and leave it out overnight. The next morning, remove the lemon and rinse the piece. If you notice any change in color in the glaze, the acid in the lemon juice was able to leach other materials out of the fired glaze. If this glaze were to be used for functional work, the acid in a cup of coffee could cause similar leaching, creating a beverage fortified with a number of unwanted ingredients. If your work fails this test, do not use that glaze on functional work. It is important to note that if your glaze passes this test, it doesn't necessarily mean that materials are not leaching out of the glaze at all, just that they are not leaching badly. If in doubt, use a stable liner glaze on all surfaces that will come into contact with food and drink, and save any questionable glazes for the exterior of your cups.

The scratch test is a quick way to tell whether silverware is likely to leave a similar mark on functional work.

Microwave test: You may also want to test your work in the microwave, as many cups, bowls, and plates will end up there at some point. Fill a test piece with water and microwave for one minute. If the clay body is not sufficiently vitrified, the water will absorb into the surface of the work and become very hot when microwaved. The expansion of this water into steam when heated can compromise the bond between the clay and glaze, causing the glaze to chip off. The thermal shock of hot water may also cause cracking if there is a misfit in the thermal expansion of the glazes on the clay, such as a tight liner on the inside and a crazed matte on the outside. Also, it should also be noted that some glazes, including lusters and other metallics, will cause sparking in a microwave and should be labeled as such when being sold or gifted.

Congratulations! At this point, you have successfully navigated the entire process of glazing. It is my hope that some of the mystery has been uncovered, and that many of the myths about glazing have been dispelled. As an Amazing Glazer, you now know how to mix a glaze just right and apply it artfully and with precision to your piece. You can fire the work carefully to get the best results and test your finished pieces for functional use. With these skills in your back pocket, you can move competently in any glaze kitchen anywhere in the world. While the recipes in the following chapter are a great starting point for your adventure, they are really just that, and the possibilities are endless. I want to wish you the best on your journey, and know that great things, and plenty of Amazing Glaze, lie ahead!

GALLERY

Woodfired Bud Vase. Micah Thanhauser.
Photo courtesy of the artist.

Wood ash deposits color the surface of this pot, while
allowing the texture of the clay itself to contribute to the
aesthetic value of the piece.

Brass Vase. John Britt. *Photo courtesy of the artist.*

Ceramic mimics brass on the surface of this bottle.

Melon Pitcher. Steven Hill. *Photo courtesy of the artist.*

No less than five glazes have been applied using a spray gun to the surface of this piece. Their interactions yield even more color combinations, including the lavender in the middle.

Pitcher. Justin Rothshank. *Photo courtesy of the artist.*

Atmospheric salt and soda enliven the surface of this tall pitcher.

Platter with Figures.
Nick Joerling.
Photo courtesy of the artist.

Masterful wax resist decoration creates a group of figures that dance across the surface of this platter.

Cloud Flared Vase. Sam Chung. *Photo courtesy of the artist.*

Careful firing leads to a flawless white surface on this uniquely shaped vase.

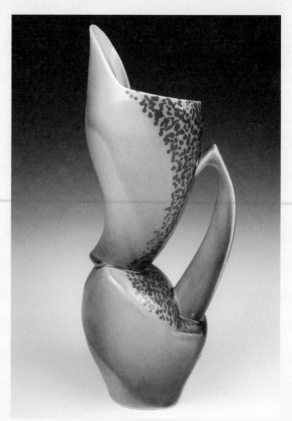

Pitcher. Deborah Schwartzkopf. *Photo courtesy of the artist.*

Encapsulated red dots work on top of a celadon glaze to provide plumage for this unique bird-shaped pitcher.

Bear Thoughts.
Taylor Robenalt.
Photo courtesy of the artist.

Gold luster and black underglaze decoration add depth and shine to the artist's porcelain work.

Black and White Jar with Handles. Sam Scott.
Photo courtesy of the artist.

Sam Scott's eye for design is impeccable. The poured teardrops of black glaze leave just enough of the white below it to create a quiet piece with big visual impact.

Bottle Vase. Bill Campbell. *Photo courtesy of the artist.*

Glaze breaking off the handles contrasts with the flowing amber base glaze and large crystals that seem to float to the top of this bulbous vase.

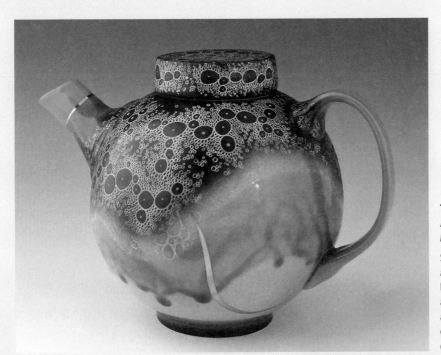

Teapot.
Adrian Sandstrom.
Photo courtesy of the artist.

Slips, underglazes, glazes, and lusters combine to build up the surface of this attractive teapot. The artist achieves a wonderful depth of surface by layering these design elements.

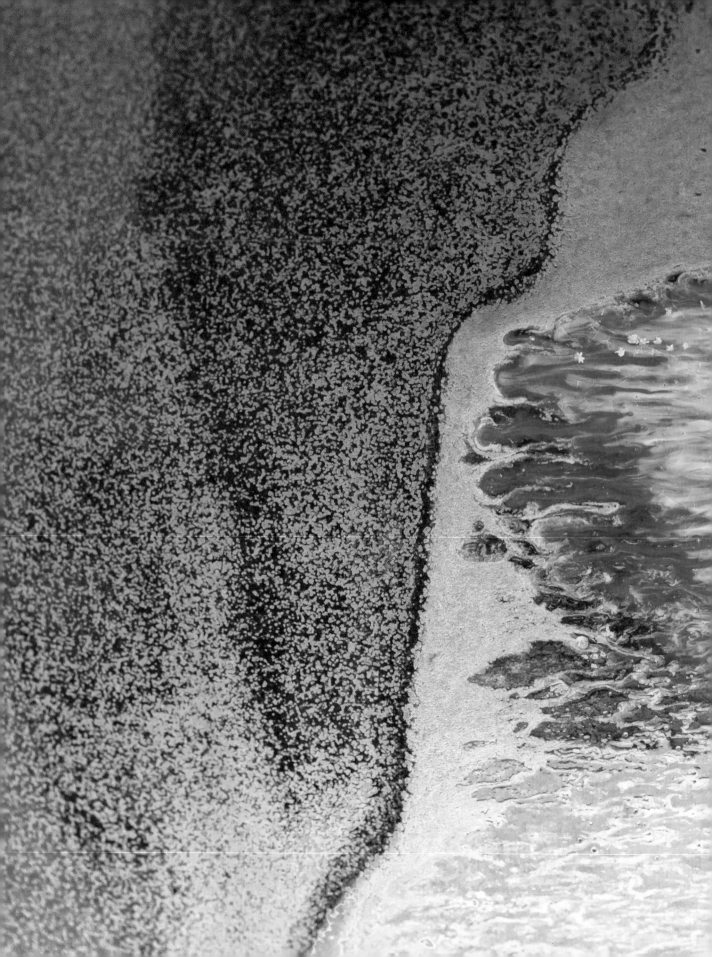

6

THE RECIPES

The Odyssey ClayWorks glaze kitchen has built an impressive array of glazes, slips, and washes over the years. The recipes have come from a number of sources: instructors, resident artists, and students have all left their mark. Some of these recipes are popular, reliable classics found in many communal studios. Others are obscure gems found through mining old texts. Still others are the result of experimentation and tweaking.

No matter the source, these glazes represent a living history, culled from dozens of workshops, hundreds of firings, and an innumerable number of tests. Credit is given to the source of the glaze whenever it is known.

Thousands of color and texture combinations are possible using these recipes. I encourage you to mix carefully, pay attention to the specific gravity (which should be 1.45 g/ml unless otherwise noted), and take detailed notes.

Happy glazing!

NOTES

- For small batches, you can round the percentages in all the recipes to the nearest whole number if your studio scale cannot measure tenths or hundredths.

- Silica comes in several mesh sizes. Use 325-mesh unless otherwise indicated.

- Laguna Borate or Gillespie Borate can be substituted for Gerstley Borate.

- All cone 10 and cone 6 glazes tests are on Highwater Clay's Helios Porcelain. Low-fire tests are on Highwater Clay's White Earthenware. If you use a different clay body, the results will vary (see page 69).

HIGH-FIRE GLAZES

AMBER CELADON

CONE: 9–10
Atmosphere: Reduction
Surface: Glossy
Color: Amber, Honey, Brown

INGREDIENTS	AMOUNTS
Alberta Slip	35.87%
Custer Feldspar	21.74%
Silica	14.13%
Wollastonite	14.13%
Whiting	7.61%
EPK	3.26%
Gerstley Borate	3.26%
TOTAL	**100.00%**

Also Add

Yellow Ochre	8.70%

BLUE CELADON

CONE: 9–10
Atmosphere: Reduction
Surface: Glossy
Color: Translucent Light Blue

INGREDIENTS	AMOUNTS
Silica	30.70%
G-200 Feldspar	29.83%
Wollastonite	23.68%
Grolleg	13.16%
Talc	2.63%
TOTAL	**100.00%**

Also Add

Red Iron Oxide	0.44%
Epsom Salt	0.25%

BECCA'S CLEAR

CONE: 10
Atmosphere: Reduction/Oxidation
Surface: Glossy
Color: Clear

INGREDIENTS	AMOUNTS
Silica	32.68%
Custer Feldspar	27.72%
EPK	19.80%
Whiting	19.80%
TOTAL	**100.00%**

Comments: From Becca Floyd.

BUTTERMILK

CONE: 9–10
Atmosphere: Reduction/Oxidation
Surface: Glossy
Color: Opaque Off-White

INGREDIENTS	AMOUNTS
Minspar	45.99%
Gerstley Borate	25.26%
OM-4 Ball Clay	15.69%
Silica	7.69%
Dolomite	5.37%
TOTAL	**100.00%**

Also Add

Zircopax	7.69%

BYRON TEMPLE SATIN MATTE

CONE: 10
Atmosphere: Reduction/Oxidation
Surface: Satin-Matte
Color: Variegated Green

INGREDIENTS	AMOUNTS
Custer Feldspar	47.57%
Cornwall Stone	17.48%
Whiting	17.48%
OM-4 Ball Clay	8.74%
EPK	5.83%
Zinc Oxide	2.90%
TOTAL	**100.00%**

Also Add

Red Iron Oxide	5.83%
Light Rutile	3.89%

OHATA KHAKI

CONE: 10
Atmosphere: Reduction
Surface: Semigloss
Color: Reddish Brown

INGREDIENTS	AMOUNTS
Custer Feldspar	51.53%
Silica	16.98%
Bone Ash	10.54%
EPK	6.67%
Talc	6.67%
Whiting	7.61%
TOTAL	**100.00%**

Also Add

Red Iron Oxide	11.36%
Bentonite	1.46%

VAL'S SATIN BLACK

CONE: 10
Atmosphere: Reduction/Oxidation
Surface: Semimatte
Color: Gunmetal Black

INGREDIENTS	AMOUNTS
Minspar	20.00%
Cornwall Stone	20.00%
Silica	20.00%
Dolomite	15.00%
Talc	13.00%
OM-4 Ball Clay	10.00%
Whiting	2.00%
TOTAL	**100.00%**

Also Add

Red Iron Oxide	3.00%
Manganese Dioxide	2.00%
Cobalt Oxide	3.00%
Chrome Oxide	1.00%

Comments: FromVal Cushing.

IPANEMA GREEN

CONE: 10
Atmosphere: Reduction/Salt/Soda
Surface: Semimatte
Color: Variegated Green

INGREDIENTS	AMOUNTS
G-200 Feldspar	47.00%
Whiting	23.00%
Dolomite	14.00%
Silica	11.00%
Bone Ash	3.50%
TOTAL	**100.00%**

Also Add

Red Iron Oxide	4.00%
Copper Carbonate	2.79%
Bentonite	2.00%

KOREAN CELADON

CONE: 9–10
Atmosphere: Reduction/Oxidation
Surface: Gloss
Color: Translucent Amber Green

INGREDIENTS	AMOUNTS
Custer Feldspar	25.85%
Whiting	25.85%
OM-4 Ball Clay	20.69%
Silica	20.69%
EPK	6.72%
Bone Ash	0.20%
TOTAL	**100.00%**

Also Add

Yellow Ochre	2.07%
Red Iron Oxide	1.55%

THE JUICE

CONE: 10
Atmosphere: Oxidation/Reduction
Surface: Crystalline Matte
Color: Off-White

INGREDIENTS	AMOUNTS
Custer Feldspar	46.24%
Whiting	17.34%
#6 Tile Kaolin	13.88%
Strontium Carbonate	12.72%
Gerstley Borate	4.62%
Lithium Carbonate	4.62%
Zinc Oxide	0.58%
TOTAL	100.00%

Also Add

Titanium Dioxide	17.34%
Bentonite	2.31%

Comments: From Hank Goodman. Inspired by Steven Hill. Not particularly attractive when used alone. This glaze works beautifully when layered with other glazes.

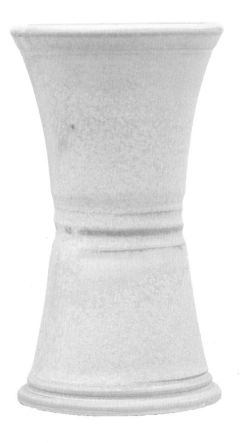

OXBLOOD

CONE: 10
Atmosphere: Reduction
Surface: Glossy
Color: Red

INGREDIENTS	AMOUNTS
Custer Feldspar	62.00%
Ferro Frit 3134	22.00%
Whiting	10.00%
EPK	4.00%
Silica	2.00%
TOTAL	100.00%

Also Add

Tin Oxide	2.00%
Copper Carbonate	1.00%
Bentonite	2.00%

Comments: From Frank Bosco.

ANJA'S SILKY CLEAR

CONE: 7–10
Atmosphere: Oxidation/Reduction
Surface: Matte
Color: Clear

INGREDIENTS	AMOUNTS
EPK	37.63%
Wollastonite	29.03%
Ferro Frit 3124	27.96%
Silica	5.38%
TOTAL	**100.00%**

Comments: Mix thin—SG 1.25. From Anja Bartels.

LINDA'S SAINT JOHN'S BLACK

CONE: 10
Atmosphere: Reduction/Oxidation
Surface: Semigloss
Color: Black

INGREDIENTS	AMOUNTS
Alberta Slip	75.00%
Nepheline Syenite	25.00%
TOTAL	**100.00%**

Also Add

Cobalt Carbonate	5.00%
Manganese Dioxide	2.00%
Bentonite	2.00%
Red Iron Oxide	1.00%
Chrome Oxide	0.25%

Comments: From Linda McFarling. Mix thick for brushwork—SG 1.80.

SCHWEIGER TURQUOISE

CONE: 10
Atmosphere: Reduction/Salt/Soda
Surface: Gloss
Color: Turquoise

INGREDIENTS	AMOUNTS
Silica	35.10%
Custer Feldspar	28.50%
Whiting	17.90%
Strontium Carbonate	9.40%
Talc	4.00%
EPK	3.20%
Bone Ash	1.90%
TOTAL	100.00%

Also Add

Copper Carbonate	3.00%
Bentonite	2.00%

REDART SHINO

CONE: 9–10
Atmosphere: Reduction
Surface: Opaque
Color: Buff to Red-Orange

INGREDIENTS	AMOUNTS
Nepheline Syenite	62.00%
OM-4 Ball Clay	17.00%
Redart Clay	9.00%
EPK	4.00%
Soda Ash	4.00%
Spodumene	4.00%
TOTAL	100.00%

Comments: Mix soda ash last. This glaze works well under any number of glazes, but poorly on top of them.

REITZ GREEN

CONE: 10
Atmosphere: Reduction
Surface: Semimatte
Color: Green/Black

INGREDIENTS	AMOUNTS
Nepheline Syenite	70.00%
Spodumene	15.00%
OM-4 Ball Clay	8.00%
Whiting	5.00%
Gerstley Borate	2.00%
TOTAL	**100.00%**

Also Add

Cobalt Carbonate	1.00%
Light Rutile	2.00%

Comments: Apply thin to medium. Thin is black. Medium is green. Rub bubbles out of raw glaze to help prevent pinholes. From Don Reitz.

TENMOKU

Cone 9–10
Atmosphere: Reduction/Oxidation
Surface: Semigloss
Color: Black/Brown

INGREDIENTS	AMOUNTS
Custer Feldspar	45.00%
Silica	27.00%
Whiting	17.00%
EPK	11.00%
TOTAL	**100.00%**

Also Add

Red Iron Oxide	10.00%

BLUE ORIBE

CONE: 9–10
Atmosphere: Reduction
Surface: Gloss
Color: Semiopaque Blue

INGREDIENTS	AMOUNTS
Custer Feldspar	30.91%
Silica	25.32%
Whiting	22.36%
EPK	12.55%
Talc	7.81%
Bone Ash	1.05%
TOTAL	**100.00%**

Also Add

Copper Carbonate	7.00%
Cobalt Carbonate	2.00%

WERTZ CARBON TRAP SHINO

CONE: 9–10
Atmosphere: Reduction
Surface: Semigloss
Color: White to Red

INGREDIENTS	AMOUNTS
Nepheline Syenite	50.00%
OM-4 Ball Clay	17.00%
Minspar	15.00%
Spodumene	12.00%
EPK	3.00%
Soda Ash	3.00%
TOTAL	**100.00%**

Also Add

Bentonite	2.00%

Comments: This glaze needs heavy reduction to trap carbon, but it is still a pleasant Shino with light reduction as shown here.

YELLOW SALT

CONE: 10–11
Atmosphere: Reduction/Salt/Soda
Surface: Glossy to Matte
Color: Opaque Light Yellow

INGREDIENTS	AMOUNTS
Nepheline Syenite	71.36%
Dolomite	23.78%
OM-4 Ball Clay	4.86%
TOTAL	**100.00%**

Also Add

Zircopax	18.03%
Red Iron Oxide	1.13%
Bentonite	4.50%
Epsom Salt (Dissolved In Water)	0.18%

Comments: From Joe Molinaro at Eastern Kentucky University. Very nice on stoneware clays. In reduction firing (no salt), it can turn a beautiful yellow matte with medium to thin application. Too-thick glaze goes shiny!

VAN GUILDER BLUE ASH

CONE: 6–10
Atmosphere: Oxidation/Reduction
Surface: Ash Rivulets
Color: Gray/Blue

INGREDIENTS	AMOUNTS
Whiting	31.00%
Tennessee #10 Ball Clay	24.00%
Silica	22.50%
Unwashed Wood Ash	15.00%
Custer Feldspar	5.00%
Dolomite	2.50%
TOTAL	**100.00%**

Also Add

Light Rutile	4.00%
Red Iron Oxide	0.75%
Cobalt Carbonate	0.50%

Comments: Ash glazes run and pool, resulting in a surface covered in rivulets. This piece was fired to cone 6.

PURPLE PASSION PLUM

CONE: 9-10
Atmosphere: Reduction
Surface: Semigloss
Color: Deep Plum

INGREDIENTS	AMOUNTS
Custer Feldspar	37.20%
Nepheline Syenite	28.00%
Ferro Frit 3134	13.20%
Whiting	8.00%
Spodumene	6.00%
OM-4 Ball Clay	3.20%
EPK	2.40%
Silica	1.20%
Gerstley Borate	0.80%
TOTAL	**100.00%**

Also Add

Bentonite	1.20%
Tin Oxide	1.20%
Light Rutile	0.80%
Copper Carbonate	0.60%
Cobalt Carbonate	0.40%

ROGER'S GREEN

CONE: 9–10
Atmosphere: Reduction
Surface: Semigloss
Color: Deep Green

INGREDIENTS	AMOUNTS
G-200 Feldspar	22.73%
Whiting	22.73%
#6 Tile	22.73%
Silica	22.73%
Strontium Carbonate	9.08%
TOTAL	**100.00%**

Also Add

Copper Carbonate	9.08%
Bentonite	1.81%

MID-RANGE GLAZES

ANJA'S KEY WEST BLUE

CONE: 6
Atmosphere: Oxidation
Surface: Glossy
Color: Variegated Turquoise

INGREDIENTS	AMOUNTS
Silica	28.86%
Minspar	18.31%
Zinc Oxide	11.94%
Custer Feldspar	10.45%
Gerstley Borate	10.25%
Whiting	6.57%
Nepheline Syenite	4.98%
EPK	4.18%
Dolomite	2.88%
Wollastonite	1.58%
TOTAL	**100.00%**

Also Add

Copper Carbonate	2.48%
Bentonite	0.60%

Comments: *From Anja Bartels.*

ALBERTA YELLOW

CONE: 5–6
Atmosphere: Oxidation
Surface: Glossy/Shiny
Color: Translucent Brown Yellow

INGREDIENTS	AMOUNTS
Alberta Slip	35.10%
Silica	23.43%
Nepheline Syenite	21.86%
Gerstley Borate	17.65%
Soda Ash	1.96%
TOTAL	**100.00%**

BROKEN CELADON

CONE: 5–6
Atmosphere: Oxidation
Surface: Semigloss
Color: Blue/Green Variation

INGREDIENTS	AMOUNTS
Gerstley Borate	50.00%
Silica	32.50%
Grolleg	17.50%
TOTAL	100.00%

Also Add

Copper Carbonate	4.00%
Light Rutile	6.00%

CHUN CELADON

CONE: 5–6
Atmosphere: Oxidation
Surface: Glossy
Color: Translucent Blue-Green

INGREDIENTS	AMOUNTS
Silica	30.00%
Minspar	38.00%
Whiting	14.00%
Zinc Oxide	12.00%
OM-4 Ball Clay	6.00%
TOTAL	100.00%

Also Add

Copper Carbonate	2.25%
Bentonite	1.00%

Comments: From Leah Leitson. This glaze is great by itself, but plays well with others. SG 1.55.

FAT CAT RED

CONE: 6
Atmosphere: Oxidation
Surface: Glossy
Color: Red

INGREDIENTS	AMOUNTS
Custer Feldspar	31.00%
Silica	18.00%
Whiting	21.00%
EPK	9.00%
Ferro Frit 3134	9.00%
Gerstley Borate	8.00%
Talc	4.00%
TOTAL	**100.00%**

Also Add

Tin Oxide	5.00%
Chrome Oxide	0.20%

COWAN AMBER

CONE: 6
Atmosphere: Oxidation
Surface: Glossy
Color: Amber

INGREDIENTS	AMOUNTS
Custer Feldspar	44.00%
Whiting	17.70%
Silica	12.80%
Redart	11.10%
OM-4 Ball Clay	6.10%
Talc	3.80%
Gerstley Borate	2.50%
Bone Ash	2.00%
TOTAL	**100.00%**

Also Add

Red Iron Oxide	4.10%

FLOATING BLUE

CONE: 6
Atmosphere: Oxidation
Surface: Glossy
Color: Blue/Brown

INGREDIENTS	AMOUNTS
Nepheline Syenite	47.30%
Gerstley Borate	27.00%
Silica	20.30%
EPK	5.40%
TOTAL	100.00%

Also Add

Light Rutile	3.00%
Cobalt Carbonate	1.50%
Red Iron Oxide	2.00%

Comments: This popular glaze works well in combination with other cone 6 glazes.

ODYSSEY CLEAR

CONE: 6
Atmosphere: Oxidation
Surface: Glossy
Color: Clear

INGREDIENTS	AMOUNTS
Silica	30.00%
Nepheline Syenite	30.00%
Gerstley Borate	20.00%
EPK	10.00%
Wollastonite	10.00%
TOTAL	100.00%

Comments: SG 1.35. From Nick Moen.

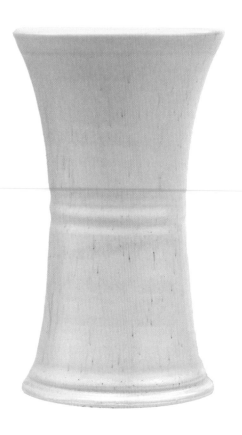

ODYSSEY WHITE GLOSS

CONE: 6
Atmosphere: Oxidation/Reduction
Surface: Glossy
Color: White

INGREDIENTS	AMOUNTS
Silica	30.00%
Nepheline Syenite	30.00%
Gerstley Borate	20.00%
EPK	10.00%
Wollastonite	10.00%
TOTAL	**100.00%**

Also Add

Zircopax	6.00%

Comments: This glaze is the same as Odyssey Clear with the addition of Zircopax to make it white and opaque. Great liner glaze that plays well with others. From Nick Moen.

GEN'S SATIN MATTE

CONE: 6
Atmosphere: Oxidation
Surface: Semimatte/Crystalline
Color: Off-White with Pink Specks

INGREDIENTS	AMOUNTS
Custer Feldspar	34.90%
Zinc Oxide	25.80%
Silica	22.60%
Whiting	12.60%
EPK	4.10%
TOTAL	**100.00%**

Also Add

Bentonite	2.00%
Light Rutile	6.50%

Comments: Semimatte when cooled slowly. Crystalline when cooled quickly. From Genevieve Van Zandt.

CHARCOAL SATIN

CONE: 6
Atmosphere: Oxidation
Surface: Semimatte
Color: Gray-Black

INGREDIENTS	AMOUNTS
EPK	31.70%
Ferro Frit 3124	31.00%
Wollastonite	23.20%
Silica	14.10%
TOTAL	**100.00%**

Also Add

Mason Stain 6650	10.00%
Dark Rutile	6.00%

MOSSY GREEN

CONE: 5–10
Atmosphere: Oxidation
Surface: Satin
Color: Green/Opaque

INGREDIENTS	AMOUNTS
Nepheline Syenite	60.00%
Strontium Carbonate	20.00%
OM-4 Ball Clay	10.00%
Silica	9.00%
Lithium Carbonate	1.00%
TOTAL	**100.00%**

Also Add

Copper Carbonate	5.00%
Titanium Dioxide	5.00%

Comments: From Pete Pinnell. Also known as Pinnell Strontium Matte or Weathered Bronze.

OL' BLUE (VARIEGATED SLATE BLUE)

CONE: 6
Atmosphere: Oxidation
Surface: Glossy
Color: Blue

INGREDIENTS	AMOUNTS
EPK	30.00%
Wollastonite	29.00%
Ferro Frit 3195	20.00%
Silica	17.00%
Nepheline Syenite	4.00%
TOTAL	**100.00%**

Also Add

Light Rutile	3.00%
Copper Carbonate	3.00%
Cobalt Carbonate	1.50%

Comments: *From John Hesselberth and Ron Roy.*

PURPLE

CONE: 6
Atmosphere: Oxidation
Surface: Matte/Semimatte/Satin
Color: Purple

INGREDIENTS	AMOUNTS
Silica	32.78%
Custer Feldspar	27.07%
Nepheline Syenite	14.39%
Whiting	12.05%
Gerstley Borate	8.44%
Lithium Carbonate	3.65%
Magnesium Carbonate	1.63%
TOTAL	**100.00%**

Also Add

Tin Oxide	4.88%
Bentonite	1.63%
Cobalt Carbonate	0.61%
Chrome Oxide	0.17%

RANDY'S RED

CONE: 6
Atmosphere: Oxidation
Surface: Semigloss
Color: Brown/Red

INGREDIENTS	AMOUNTS
Gerstley Borate	32.00%
Silica	30.00%
Minspar	20.00%
Talc	14.00%
EPK	4.00%
TOTAL	**100.00%**

Also Add

Red Iron Oxide	15.00%

Comments: *A slower firing will result in more variation on the surface, including red brown speckles. A faster firing will result in a dark red/brown, as shown here.*

SILKY BLACK

CONE: 6
Atmosphere: Oxidation
Surface: Semigloss
Color: Black

INGREDIENTS	AMOUNTS
Nepheline Syenite	33.11%
Minspar	16.79%
EPK	12.57%
Silica	7.97%
Gerstley Borate	7.50%
Whiting	7.13%
Zinc Oxide	6.19%
Talc	5.45%
Dolomite	3.29%
TOTAL	**100.00%**

Also Add

Black Copper Oxide	5.63%
Red Iron Oxide	5.63%
Cobalt Oxide	1.88%

BRITT'S PRETTY MATTE MUSTARD

CONE: 6
Atmosphere: Oxidation
Surface: Matte
Color: Yellow

INGREDIENTS	AMOUNTS
Custer Feldspar	48.10%
Ferro Frit 3134	12.70%
Dolomite	24.00%
EPK	10.40%
Whiting	4.80%
TOTAL	**100.00%**

Also Add

Titanium Dioxide	10.00%
Nickel Oxide	2.20%
Bentonite	2.00%

Comments: From John Britt.

SPEARMINT

CONE: 5–6
Atmosphere: Oxidation
Surface: Semisatin
Color: Green

INGREDIENTS	AMOUNTS
Wollastonite	28.00%
EPK	28.00%
Ferro Frit 3195	23.00%
Silica	17.00%
Nepheline Syenite	4.00%
TOTAL	**100.00%**

Also Add

Light Rutile	6.00%
Copper Carbonate	4.00%

Comments: From John Hesselberth and Ron Roy.

STRONTIUM CRYSTAL MAGIC

CONE: 6
Atmosphere: Oxidation
Surface: Matte crystalline
Color: Off-White

INGREDIENTS	AMOUNTS
Custer Feldspar	46.00%
Whiting	17.20%
#6 Tile	14.90%
Strontium Carbonate	12.70%
Lithium Carbonate	4.60%
Ferro Frit 3124	4.60%
TOTAL	**100.00%**

Also Add

Titanium Dioxide	12.00%
Bentonite	2.00%

Comments: From Steven Hill. This glaze should be used only as a modifier glaze. It will add white crystals that float in the surface of the other glazes. It can be very runny, so only apply to the top third of the piece, and make sure to use kiln cookies.

STEPHAN'S STRONTIUM

CONE: 5–6
Atmosphere: Oxidation
Surface: Waxy Rich Satin Matte
Color: Aqua Green with Black if Thick

INGREDIENTS	AMOUNTS
Nepheline Syenite	57.30%
Strontium Carbonate	27.08%
Lithium Carbonate	2.08%
Silica	7.29%
EPK	6.25%
TOTAL	**100.00%**

Also Add

Copper Carbonate	4–10.00%
Epsom Salt	0.25%

Comments: Crusty black where 10% Copper Carbonate is used. 4% Copper Carbonate (shown here) gives a green tone. Nice waxy white matte with no colorants.

CHAMELEON GRAY-GREEN

CONE: 5–6
Atmosphere: Oxidation
Surface: Semimatte
Color: Green/Gray

INGREDIENTS	AMOUNTS
Minspar	50.00%
EPK	20.00%
Talc	15.00%
Whiting	10.00%
Zinc Oxide	10.00%
Lithium Carbonate	2.00%
TOTAL	**100.00%**

Also Add

Copper Carbonate	3.00%

Comments: This glaze works best on porcelain/white clay. Thick application produces mottled gray; thin application produces smooth aqua.

TURQUOISE MATTE

CONE: 6
Atmosphere: Oxidation
Surface: Matte
Color: Turquoise Blue-Green

INGREDIENTS	AMOUNTS
Nepheline Syenite	70.75%
Strontium Carbonate	26.78%
Gerstley Borate	2.47%
TOTAL	**100.00%**

Also Add

Copper Carbonate	3.91%
Bentonite	2.88%

LOW-FIRE GLAZES

BUMBY'S BEADS

CONE: 05–04
Atmosphere: Oxidation
Surface: Crawl
Color: White

INGREDIENTS	AMOUNTS
Magnesium Carbonate	34.04%
Gerstley Borate	32.98%
Borax	26.60%
Silica	6.38%
TOTAL	**100.00%**

Also Add
Zircopax	6.38%

Comments: Bumby's Beads is a crawl glaze. Alligator skin texture, but not recommended for functional work.

CASSIE'S BLING

CONE: 05–04
Atmosphere: Oxidation
Surface: Textured Crystal
Color: White

INGREDIENTS	AMOUNTS
Magnesium Carbonate	35.00%
Cryolite (Toxic)	30.00%
Lithium Carbonate	25.00%
Borax	10.00%
TOTAL	**100.00%**

Also Add
Mason Stain 6023	6.60%

Comments: Crawl glaze. From Cassie Ryalls Butcher.

JACKIE'S BLUE

CONE: 05–04
Atmosphere: Oxidation
Surface: Semimatte
Color: Turquoise

INGREDIENTS	AMOUNTS
Silica	42.00%
Gerstley Borate	38.00%
Lithium Carbonate	10.00%
Nepheline Syenite	5.00%
EPK	5.00%
TOTAL	**100.00%**

Also Add

Bentonite	2.00%
Cobalt Carbonate	2.00%

JACKIE'S TURQUOISE

CONE: 05–04
Atmosphere: Oxidation
Surface: Semimatte
Color: Turquoise

INGREDIENTS	AMOUNTS
Silica	42.00%
Gerstley Borate	38.00%
Lithium Carbonate	10.00%
Nepheline Syenite	5.00%
EPK	5.00%
TOTAL	**100.00%**

Also Add

Copper Carbonate	3.00%
Bentonite	2.00
Red Iron Oxide	1.00%

JOHN'S BLUE

CONE: 05–04
Atmosphere: Oxidation
Surface: Translucent Gloss
Color: Blue-Turquoise

INGREDIENTS	AMOUNTS
Ferro Frit 3110	77.00%
Silica	10.00%
EPK	7.00%
Gerstley Borate	6.00%
TOTAL	**100.00%**

Also Add

Copper Carbonate	2.00%

LEE'S BLACK

CONE: 05–04
Atmosphere: Oxidation
Surface: Semimatte/Satin
Color: Black

INGREDIENTS	AMOUNTS
Ferro Frit 3124	30.00%
Gerstley Borate	26.00%
Nepheline Syenite	20.00%
Lithium Carbonate	4.00%
EPK	10.00%
Silica	10.00%
TOTAL	**100.00%**

Also Add

Mason Stain 6650	10.00%

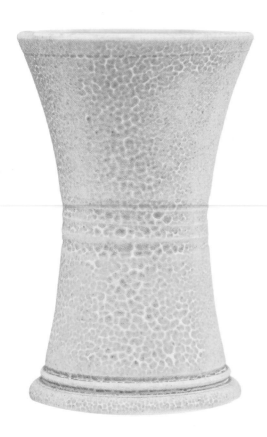

LIZARD

CONE: 05–04
Atmosphere: Oxidation
Surface: Crawl
Color: Semiopaque Brown/Yellow

INGREDIENTS	AMOUNTS
Gerstley Borate	43.54%
Nepheline Syenite	12.44%
Silica	3.10%
Borax	6.22%
Magnesium Carbonate	25.38%
Lithium Carbonate	9.32%
TOTAL	**100.00%**

Also Add

Red Iron Oxide	3.96%

SPARKLE

CONE: 05–04
Atmosphere: Oxidation
Surface: Glossy
Color: Brown and Amber

INGREDIENTS	AMOUNTS
Ferro Frit 3124	30.00%
Gerstley Borate	26.00%
Lithium Carbonate	4.00%
Nepheline Syenite	20.00%
EPK	10.00%
Imsil 400m Silica	10.00%
TOTAL	**100.00%**

Also Add

Yellow Ochre	5.00%
Spanish Red Iron Oxide	4.00%
Manganese Dioxide	1.00%

VC SATIN STONE

CONE: 05–04
Atmosphere: Oxidation
Surface: Opaque Satin
Color: White

INGREDIENTS	AMOUNTS
Ferro Frit 3124	44.12%
Silica	14.71%
Nepheline Syenite	14.71%
Gerstley Borate	9.80%
Talc	4.90%
Whiting	4.90%
EPK	4.90%
Zinc Oxide	1.96%
TOTAL	**100.00%**

Comments: From Val Cushing.

VC SATIN ROBIN'S EGG BLUE

CONE: 05–04
Atmosphere: Oxidation
Surface: Opaque Satin
Color: White

INGREDIENTS	AMOUNTS
Ferro Frit 3124	44.12%
Silica	14.71%
Nepheline Syenite	14.71%
Gerstley Borate	9.80%
Talc	4.90%
Whiting	4.90%
EPK	4.90%
Zinc Oxide	1.96%
TOTAL	**100.00%**

Also Add

Mason Stain 6376	4.90%
Copper Carbonate	0.98%

Comments: From Val Cushing.

WARM CLEAR

CONE: 05–04
Atmosphere: Oxidation/Reduction
Surface: Semigloss
Color: Clear

INGREDIENTS	AMOUNTS
Gerstley Borate	55.00%
EPK	30.00%
Flint	15.00%
TOTAL	**100.00%**

Also Add

Rutile	1.50%

RAKU GLAZES

Glazes in this section should only be used with *raku* firing (see pages 115 to 117).

STEVE LOUCK'S *RAKU* CRACKLE

CONE: 06
Atmosphere: Oxidation/Reduction
Surface: Glossy Crackle
Color: Clear

INGREDIENTS	AMOUNTS
Gerstley Borate	37.21%
Ferro Frit 3110	37.21%
Nepheline Syenite	18.60%
EPK	6.98%
TOTAL	**100.00%**

Comments: Best crackle effect when applied thick. 3mm is recommended.

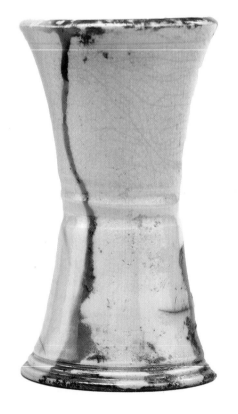

BURGUNDY MATTE

CONE: 04
Atmosphere: Oxidation/Reduction
Surface: Matte
Color: Burgundy

INGREDIENTS	AMOUNTS
Gerstley Borate	50.00%
Talc	30.00%
Nepheline Syenite	20.00%
TOTAL	**100.00%**

Also Add

Copper Carbonate	3.00%
Bentonite	2.00%

Comments: *Best when thin, goes green when applied thick.*

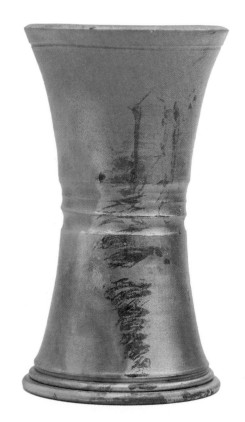

RICK'S BLUE RED

CONE: 04
Atmosphere: Oxidation/Reduction
Surface: Shiny
Color: Blue Red Flash

INGREDIENTS	AMOUNTS
Gerstley Borate	49.03%
Lithium Carbonate	25.75%
Spodumene	25.22%
TOTAL	**100.00%**

Also Add

Zircopax	23.84%
Copper Carbonate	1.61%
Cobalt Carbonate	1.61%
Epsom Salt	0.76%

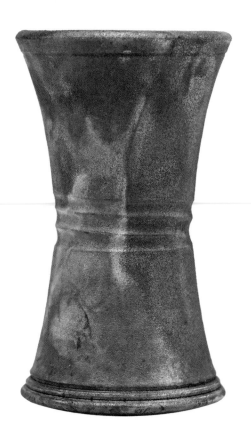

ALLIGATOR *RAKU*

CONE: 04
Atmosphere: Oxidation/Reduction
Surface: Crawl
Color: Blue-Green

INGREDIENTS	AMOUNTS
Gerstley Borate	66.67%
Bone Ash	33.33%
TOTAL	**100.00%**

Also Add

Copper Carbonate	8.33%
Cobalt Carbonate	8.33%

RICK'S TURQUOISE

CONE: 04
Atmosphere: Oxidation/Reduction
Surface: Shiny
Color: Turquoise

INGREDIENTS	AMOUNTS
Gerstley Borate	39.81%
Lithium Carbonate	20.49%
Spodumene	20.10%
Nepheline Syenite	19.70%
TOTAL	**100.00%**

Also Add

Zircopax	18.99%
Copper Carbonate	2.51%
Epsom Salt	0.61%

PALE LEMON LUSTRE

CONE: 04
Atmosphere: Oxidation/Reduction
Surface: Glossy
Color: Yellow

INGREDIENTS	AMOUNTS
Gerstley Borate	75.00%
Soda Feldspar	25.00%
TOTAL	**100.00%**

Also Add

Copper Carbonate	3.00%
Manganese Dioxide	1.50%
Bentonite	2.00%

PIEPENBURG CRACKLE

CONE: 04
Atmosphere: Oxidation/Reduction
Surface: Crackle
Color: White

INGREDIENTS	AMOUNTS
Gerstley Borate	70.00%
Nepheline Syenite	20.00%
Flint	10.00%
TOTAL	**100.00%**

Comments: Best crackle effect when applied thick. 3mm is recommended.

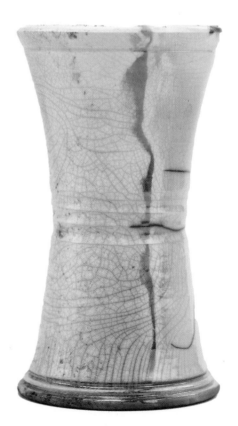

SLIPS

Apply all slips to leather-hard clay unless otherwise noted.

BAUER SLIP

CONE: 6–10

INGREDIENTS	AMOUNTS
EPK	50.00%
OM-4 Ball Clay	50.00%
TOTAL	100.00%

Also Add

Zircopax	1.25%
Borax	0.65%

BAUER ORANGE SLIP

CONE: 6–10

INGREDIENTS	AMOUNTS
EPK	46.93%
OM-4 Ball Clay	46.93%
Borax	6.14%
TOTAL	100.00%

Also Add

Zircopax	11.73%

HELMER FLASHING SLIP

CONE: 6–10

INGREDIENTS	AMOUNTS
Helmer Kaolin	50.00%
EPK	20.00%
Nepheline Syenite	20.00%
Silica	10.00%
TOTAL	100.00%

Also Add

Bentonite	2.00%

Comments: Looks good in salt/soda.

MATT LONG BUTTER SLIP

CONE: 6–10

INGREDIENTS	AMOUNTS
Grolleg Kaolin	88.89%
Borax	11.11%
TOTAL	100.00%

Also Add

Zircopax	11.11%
Titanium Dioxide	8.88%

Comments: Apply thinly to bisque. Soak borax in water until dissolved before using recipe.

LITE AVERY SLIP

CONE: 6–10

INGREDIENTS	AMOUNTS
Helmer Kaolin	48.78%
Custer Feldspar	21.94%
OM-4 Ball Clay	14.64%
Silica	14.64%
TOTAL	100.00%

Also Add

Bentonite	2.43%

RED SLIP

CONE: 6–10

INGREDIENTS	AMOUNTS
Helmer Kaolin	63.73%
Grolleg Kaolin	19.60%
Nepheline Syenite	14.71%
Borax	1.96%
TOTAL	100.00%

Also Add

Bentonite	1.96%

TRAILING SLIP FOR BISQUE

CONE: 6–10

INGREDIENTS	AMOUNTS
Custer Feldspar	70.00%
OM-4 Ball Clay	20.00%
Talc	10.00%
TOTAL	100.00%

Comments: Apply to bisqueware.

TILE #6 SLIP

CONE: 6–10

INGREDIENTS	AMOUNTS
#6 Tile	70.00%
Nepheline Syenite	30.00%
TOTAL	100.00%

Also Add

Bentonite	3.00%

POOR MAN'S PORCELAIN SLIP

CONE: 04–6

INGREDIENTS	AMOUNTS
Silica	25.00%
G-200 Feldspar	25.00%
EPK	25.00%
OM-4 Ball Clay	25.00%
TOTAL	100.00%

FISH SAUCE SLIP

CONE: 04–10

INGREDIENTS	AMOUNTS
EPK	43.70%
Silica	15.60%
Minspar	23.50%
Bentonite	9.40%
Pyrotrol	7.80%
TOTAL	100.00%

For Black Also Add

Red Iron Oxide	3.00%
Cobalt Carbonate	2.00%
Manganese Dioxide	2.00%

For Blue Also Add

Cobalt Carbonate	2.00%

For Green Also Add

Copper Carbonate	3.00%

OESTRICH SLIP

CONE: 04–10

INGREDIENTS	AMOUNTS
#6 Tile	40.00%
OM-4 Ball Clay	30.00%
Silica 200M	15.00%
Custer Feldspar	15.00%
TOTAL	100.00%

WOLKOW SLIP

CONE: 05–2

INGREDIENTS	AMOUNTS
EPK	40.00%
OM-4 Ball Clay	30.00%
Custer Feldspar	15.00%
Silica	15.00%
TOTAL	**100.00%**

For Off-White Also Add

Light Rutile	4.00%

For Yellow Also Add

Mason Stain 2022	10.00%

For Blue Also Add

Cobalt Carbonate	4.00%

For Green Also Add

Copper Carbonate	3.00%

RED ORANGE FLASHING SLIP

CONE: 10

INGREDIENTS	AMOUNTS
Helmer Kaolin	50.00%
EPK	20.00%
Nepheline Syenite	20.00%
Silica	10.00%
TOTAL	**100.00%**

Also Add

Bentonite	2.00%

UNDERGLAZES, WASHES, TERRA SIGILLATAS, AND OTHER RECIPES

ODYSSEY 1/1/1 UNDERGLAZE

CONE: 04–10

INGREDIENTS	AMOUNTS
EPK	33.34%
Ferro Frit 3124	33.33%
Stain or Oxide	33.33%
TOTAL	100.00%

COBALT WASH

CONE: 06–10

INGREDIENTS	AMOUNTS
Ferro Frit 3124	50.00%
EPK	50.00%
TOTAL	100.00%

Also Add

Cobalt Carbonate	25.00%

RED IRON WASH

CONE: 06–10

INGREDIENTS	AMOUNTS
Ferro Frit 3124	50.00%
EPK	50.00%
TOTAL	100.00%

Also Add

Red Iron Oxide	50.00%

COBALT IRON WASH

CONE: 06–10

INGREDIENTS	AMOUNTS
Ferro Frit 3124	50.00%
EPK	50.00%
TOTAL	100.00%

Also Add

Cobalt Carbonate	50.00%
Red Iron Oxide	50.00%

COPPER OXIDE WASH

CONE: 06–10

INGREDIENTS	AMOUNTS
Ferro Frit 3124	50.00%
EPK	50.00%
TOTAL	100.00%

Also Add

Copper Carbonate	50.00%

RED ART TERRA SIG

CONE: 04

INGREDIENTS	AMOUNTS
Red Art Clay	20.00%
Water	80.00%
TOTAL	100.00%

Also Add

Sodium Silicate	2.35%

Comments: *Mix ingredients in a blender. Allow to materials to settle out and separate for 24–48 hours. Siphon off the middle of the three layers. Use this material as you would a slip. Can be burnished for additional effect.*

KILN WASH

INGREDIENTS	AMOUNTS
Alumina Hydrate	50.00%
Glomax	25.00%
EPK	25.00%
TOTAL	100.00%

WADDING

INGREDIENTS	AMOUNTS
EPK	50.00%
Alumina Hydrate	50.00%
TOTAL	100.00%

RESOURCES

RECOMMENDED READING

The Art of Crystalline Glazing: Basic Techniques, Jon Price and LeRoy Price

Ash Glazes, Robert Tichane

The Ceramic Spectrum, A Simplified Approach to Glaze and Color Development, Robin Hopper

Clay and Glazes for the Potter, Daniel Rhodes

The Complete Guide to High-Fire Glazes: Glazing and Firing at Cone 10, John Britt

The Complete Guide to Mid-Range Glazes: Glazing and Firing at Cones 4–7, John Britt

The Complete Potter's Companion, Tony Birks

Electric Kiln Ceramics: A Guide to Clays and Glazes, Richard Zakin

Finding One's Way with Clay: Pinched Pottery and the Color of Clay, Paulus Berensohn

Glazes Cone 6: 1240°C/2264°F, Michael Bailey

Glazes for Special Effects, Herbert H. Sanders

Image Transfer on Clay: Screen, Relief, Decal, and Monoprint Techniques, Paul Andrew Wandless

Mary Rogers on Pottery and Porcelain: A Hand-builder's Approach, Mary Rogers

Mastering Cone 6 Glazes: Improving Durability, Fit, and Aesthetics, John Hesselberth and Ron Roy

The Potter's Complete Book of Clay and Glazes, James Chappell

The Potter's Complete Studio Handbook: The Essential, Start-to-Finish Guide for Ceramic Artists, Kristin Muller and Jeff Zamek

The Potter's Palette: A Practical Guide to Creating Over 700 Illustrated Glaze and Slip Colors, Christine Constant and Steve Ogden

Raku Art and Technique, Hal Riegger

Raku Pottery, Robert Piepenburg

Reds, Reds, Copper Reds, Robert Tichane

Salt-Glazed Ceramics, Jack Troy

Smashing Glazes: 53 Artists Share Insights and Recipes, Susan Peterson

Those Celadon Blues, Robert Tichane

CERAMIC SUPPLIERS

Aardvark Clay and Supplies, Santa Ana, CA
www.aardvarkclay.com

American Art Clay Company (Amaco), Indianapolis, IN
www.amaco.com

Axner Pottery Supply, Oviedo, FL
www.axner.com

Bailey Ceramic Supplies and Equipment, Kingston, NY
www.baileypottery.com

Big Ceramic Store, Sparks, NV
www.bigceramicstore.com

Bluebird Manufacturing, Fort Collins, CO
www.bluebird-mfg.com

Clay King, Spartanburg, SC
www.clay-king.com

DiamondCore Tools, El Cajon, CA
www.diamondcoretools.com

Geil Kilns, Huntington Beach, CA
www.kilns.com

Highwater Clays, Asheville, NC
www.highwaterclays.com

Laguna Clay Company, City of Industry, CA
www.lagunaclay.com

L&L Manufacturing, Swedesboro, NJ
www.hotkilns.com

Sheffield Pottery, Sheffield, MA
www.sheffield-pottery.com

Shimpo Ceramics, Glendale Heights, IL
www.shimpoceramics.com

Standard Ceramic Supply Company, Pittsburgh, PA
www.standardceramic.com

CERAMIC ART CENTERS

Anderson Ranch Arts Center,
Snowmass Village, CA
www.andersonranch.org

Beatrice Wood Center for the Arts, Ojai, CA
www.beatricewood.com

Archie Bray Foundation for the Ceramic Arts,
Helena, MT
www.archibray.org

Armory Art Center, West Palm Beach, FL
www.armoryart.org

Arrowmont School of Arts and Crafts,
Gatlinburg, TN
www.arrowmont.org

Baltimore Clayworks, Baltimore, MD
www.baltimoreclayworks.org

Carbondale Clay Center, Carbondale, CO
www.carbondaleclay.org

Center for Craft, Creativity, and Design,
Asheville, NC
www.craftcreativitydesign.org

The Clay Studio, Philadelphia, PA
www.theclaystudio.org

Greenwich House Pottery, New York, NY
www.greenwichhouse.org/gh_pottery

Harvard Ceramics Program, Allston, MA
www.ofa.fas.harvard.edu/ceramics

Haystack Mountain School of Crafts,
Deer Isle, ME
www.haystack-mtn.org

John C. Campbell Folk School, Brasstown, NC
www.folkschool.com

Lillstreet Art Center, Chicago, IL
www.lillstreet.com

Mendocino Art Center, Mendocino, CA
www.mendocinoartcenter.org

Morean Arts Center, Saint Petersburg, FL
www.moreanartscenter.org

Northern Clay Center, Minneapolis, MN
www.northernclaycenter.org

Odyssey ClayWorks, Asheville, NC
www.odysseyclayworks.com

Penland School of Crafts, Penland, NC
www.penland.org

Pewabic Pottery, Detroit, MI
www.pewabic.org

Pottery Northwest, Seattle, WA
www.potterynorthwest.org

Red Lodge Clay Center, Red Lodge, MT
www.redlodgeclaycenter.com

Red Star Studios, Kansas City, MO
www.redstarstudios.org

Santa Fe Clay, Santa Fe, NM
www.santafeclay.com

Watershed Center for the Ceramic Arts,
Newcastle, ME
www.watershedceramics.org

Worcester Center for Crafts, Worcester, MA
www.worcestercraftcenter.org

PRINT AND ONLINE PUBLICATIONS

American Craft Council
www.craftcouncil.org

Ceramic Arts Daily
www.ceramicartsdaily.com

Ceramic Review
www.ceramicreview.com

Ceramics: Art and Perception/Ceramics
Technical
www.ceramicart.com.au

Ceramics Monthly
www.ceramicsartsdaily.org/ceramics-monthly

CFile
www.cfileonline.org

Pottery Making Illustrated
www.ceramicsartsdaily.org/pottery-making-
illustrated

Studio Potter Journal
www.thestudiopotterjournal.tumblr.com

ACKNOWLEDGMENTS

As the saying goes, "Many hands make light work." The writing of this book would not have been possible without the efforts of a number of wonderful people. Thom O'Hearn and Michael Kline spent countless hours helping me hone the content of the text with their superb editorial skills. John Britt's legendary technical expertise has been an invaluable asset during the writing of this book, and he has been incredibly generous with his time. Tim Robison's photography jumps off the pages. Thank you for understanding the aesthetic vision behind the book. It looks amazing! Anja Bartels beautifully threw all the tumblers for the glaze samples. Ananda Springsteen and Rebecca Kline provided much needed counsel during the more stressful periods of the past year, even at the oddest hours of early morning. Special thanks go out to Brian and Gail McCarthy, for their mentorship and continued support of the Odyssey family. Finally, I would like to thank the talented staff at Odyssey ClayWorks, and all of the remarkable artists who contributed images for this book. Your work is an inspiration to me and keeps me motivated to push forward in the field of ceramics. My heartfelt thanks to you all.

INDEX

A

air gun, 31
Alberta Yellow, 170
Alligator *Raku*, 188
Almeda, Jon, 90
alumina hydrate, 79
Amber Celadon, 158
Anja's Key West Blue, 170
Anja's Silky Clear, 30, 164
applying glaze
   about, 39
   basic application, 44–53
   layering glazes, 55–61
   plan for, 40–41
   single coats, 54
   troubleshooting, 62
ash firing, 118
ATP enhancer, 146

B

Ballek, Sara, 41, 92
banding wheels, 18
Bartels, Anja, 82–84
base glaze, 21
basic application, 44–53
batch size, adjusting, 23–24
Bauer Orange Slip, 190
Bauer Slip, 190
Becca's Clear, 159
bisque, prepping, 31
bisque firing, 132–135
Black-Tie Affair, 56
bloop, 48
Blue Celadon, 159
Blue Oribe, 167
blunger attachment, 18
Britt, John, 22, 34, 152
Britt's Pretty Matte Mustard, 178
Broken Celadon, 171
brushes, 18, 79
brushing, 50–51, 87
buckets, 16
building depth, 68–76
Bumby's Beads, 181
Burgundy Matte, 187
Buttermilk, 60–61, 160
Byron Temple Satin Matte, 160

C

Campbell, Bill, 128, 155
candling, 132
Carter, Ben, 35, 64, 93
Cash, Naim, 73, 80, 113–114
Cassie's Bling, 148, 181
ceramic art centers, 195
ceramic suppliers, 194
Chameleon Gray-Green, 144, 180
channel lock tongs, 18, 48
Charcoal Satin, 54, 56, 175
chemistry of glazes, 21–22
china paints, 106, 108
Christmas Red, 99
Chun Celadon, 30, 51, 56–58, 83, 98, 144, 171
Chung, Sam, 36, 64, 92, 154
Clay and Glazes for the Potter (Rhodes), 22
clay body, color of, 69
cleaning up, after firing, 145
Cobalt Iron Wash, 193
Cobalt Wash, 193
coloring oxides, 22–23
combining glazes, 32–33
commercial glazes, 26
commercial underglazes, 74–75
Complete Guide to High-Fire Glazes (Britt), 22
Complete Guide to Mid-Range Glazes (Britt), 22
Concerning the Spiritual in Art (Kandinsky), 40
cones, 24
consistency, changing, 30–31
Cook, Tisha, 138–139
cookies, 55, 137, 138–139
Copper Oxide Wash, 193
Copper Red Glazes (Tichane), 98
copper reds, 98
Copus, Josh, 119–121
Cornish-Keefe, Evan, 127, 129
cost, 26
Cowan Amber, 172
cracking, 62
crawling, 148

crazing, 149
Crystal Magic, 56–58
crystalline glazes, 100–105

D

dampers, 142
Daunis, Nick, 35
decals, 106–108, 110–111
delicate work, glazing, 90
density, 28
depth, building, 68–76
depth gauges, 44–45
Desert Sunrise, 59
design efficiency, 15–16
diamond sanding disk, 145–146
dipping, 46–48, 87–88
down fire program, 140
Dremel tool, 145, 146
drills, 16, 18
dry glazing, 86
dunting, 148
durability, 150–151
dust mask, 13, 16, 19, 27, 31, 52, 86, 112, 145

E

Edgar Plastic Kaolin (EPK), 21–22
encapsulated reds, 99
engobes, 70
environmental impact, 13
eutectic, 55

F

Fat Cat Red, 57, 98, 172
featured artists
   Bartels, Anja, 82–84
   Cash, Naim, 113–114
   Cook, Tisha, 138–139
   Copus, Josh, 119–121
   Kolstad, Cayce, 42–43
   McFarling, Linda, 122–124
   Moen, Nick, 102–104
   Morning-glory, Molly, 113–114
   Weber, Julia Claire, 110–111
"finger dip" method, 28
Fire Engine Red, 99
Firelake, 57
firing, 132–137

firing range, 143–144
firing schedules, 134–135, 140, 142
Fish Sauce Slip, 74, 144, 191
Floating Blue, 173
flux, 21–23
Forest Meets the Beach, 59
freezer test, 144, 150
funnels, 18

G

galleries, 34–37, 63–65, 91–95, 125–129, 152–155
Gen's Satin Matte, 100, 102–103, 174
Gholson, Bruce, 126–127
glass former, 21–23
glaze design, 40–41
glaze firing, 136–137, 140–141
glaze kitchen
    about, 12
    efficient design for, 15–16
    role of, 11
    safety in, 13
    tools and materials in, 16–19
    waste in, 13–14
glaze taxis, 15, 16
grinding, 145–146
guard cone, 24
guide cone, 24

H

Harris, Laurie Caffery, 37, 68, 75, 93
heat work, 24, 26
Helmer Flashing Slip, 190
Henneke, Samantha, 127
Hesselberth, John, 54
HG Raven, 161
high-fire glaze recipes, 158–169
Hill, Steven, 35, 63, 92, 153
horizontal form, dipping, 48
hydrometer, 18, 28–30

I

incised lines, 68
in-glaze painting, 51
Ipanema Green, 162

J

Jackie's Blue, 182
Jackie's Turquoise, 182
Joerling, Nick, 36, 64, 91, 153

John's Blue, 183
Jones, Maggie and Freeman, 113
Juice, The, 55, 60–61, 100, 163

K

Kandinsky, Wassily, 40
kiln atmosphere, 26
kiln shelves, 132
kiln sitters, 140
kiln wash, 136–137, 193
Kline, Gabriel, 144
Kline, Michael, 79
Knoche, Eric, 106
Kolstad, Cayce, 42–43, 141
Korean Celadon, 162

L

ladling glaze, 85
large work
    firing, 135
    glazing, 87–89
latex, 80
layering glazes, 55–61, 79
Lee, Cynthia, 71–72
Lee's Black, 183
lemon test, 144, 150
Life on Mars, 60
Linda's Saint John's Black, 164
line blends, 32–33
Lite Avery Slip, 190
Lizard, 184
low-fire glaze recipes, 170–180
lusters, 106, 109

M

mason stains, 22–23
Mastering Cone 6 Glaze (Roy and Hesselberth), 54
materials
    conscious use of, 13
    storage for, 13, 15
Matt Long Butter Slip, 190
McCusker, Mac Star, 91
McFarling, Linda, 122–124
"meaningful" test tiles, 32
microwave test, 144, 151
Midnight in Maine, 58
mid-range glaze recipes, 170–180
mixing, 27
mixing your own glazes, commercial versus, 26
Moen, Nick, 100–101

Morning-glory, Molly, 80, 112–114
Mossy Green, 175

N

non-glaze finishes, 112–114

O

Oasis, 56
Odyssey 1/1/1 Underglaze, 193
Odyssey Clear, 30, 73, 173
Odyssey White Gloss, 56, 69, 174
Oestrich Slip, 191
Ohata Khaki, 60, 161
Ol' Blue, 57–58, 176
Oxblood, 60, 98, 163
oxidation, 25, 142
oxiprobe, 142

P

Pale Lemon Lustre, 189
personal aesthetic, 41
physical water, 132
Piepenburg Crackle, 189
pinholing, 146–147
Pinnell, Pete, 140
Pisgah Forest, 57
pitchers, 18
plan, forming, 40–41
plastic wrap resist technique, 82–84
Poor Man's Porcelain Slip, 191
pouring, 49, 87, 89
preparing to glaze, 27–31
prepping work to be glazed, 31
publications, 195
Purple, 176
Purple Passion Plum, 42, 59, 61, 98, 169

Q

quadraxial blends, 33
quartz inversion, 134

R

Radiant Red, 98, 99
Rainbow Waterfall Forest, 8–9, 61
raku, 115–118, 186–189
Randy's Red, 177
recipes
    adjusting, 23
    high-fire glazes, 158–169

how to read, 22–23
kiln wash, 193
low-fire glazes, 181–186
mid-range glazes, 170–180
raku glazes, 186–189
slip, 190–192
terra sigillata, 193
underglazes, 193
wadding, 193
washes, 193
Red Art Terra Sig, 193
Red Iron Wash, 193
Red Orange Flashing Slip, 192
Red Slip, 190
Redart Shino, 165
reds, 98–99
reduction firing, 25, 141–143
refractories, 21
Reitz Green, 61, 166
resists, 77–84
resources, 194
respirator, 13, 16, 19, 27, 31, 52, 86, 112, 145
Rhodes, Daniel, 22
Rick's Blue Red, 187
Rick's Turquoise, 188
Robenalt, Taylor, 37, 93, 109, 126, 154
Roger's Green, 59, 141, 169
Rothshank, Justin, 153
Roy, Ron, 54

S

safety, 13
safety data sheet (SDS), 16
salt firing, 115, 118, 122–124
sandblasters, 112
Sandstrom, Adrian, 37, 65, 99, 129, 155
Saxe, Adrian, 106
Schwartzkof, Deborah, 37, 65, 95, 154
Schweiger Turquoise, 165
Scott, Sam, 63, 65, 94, 155
scratch test, 144, 150–151
Seger formula, 22
sgraffito, 82
shivering, 149
sieves, 18
sieving, 28
Silky Black, 177
single coats, 54
slaking, 27

slip, 70, 73, 82, 190–192
small work, glazing, 90
Snorkeling in Saint John, 58
soda firing, 115, 118
Sparkle, 54, 184
Spearmint, 20–21, 22–23, 24, 51, 54, 57, 144, 178
specific gravity (SG), 18, 28–31, 44, 46
sponging, 86
spraying, 52–53, 87
stabilizer, 21–23
stains, 76
stencils, 81
Stephan's Strontium, 179
Steve Louck's *Raku* Crackle, 186
stickers, 81
stir sticks, 16, 18
Strontium Crystal Magic, 55, 58, 60–61, 83, 100, 179

T

tape, 80
target cone, 24
Tassistro, Angelique, 94
temperature, 24
Tenmoku, 54, 166
terra sigillata, 70–72, 193
testing durability, 150–151
testing glazes, 32–33
Thanhauser, Micah, 76, 152
Tichane, Robert, 98
Tile #6 Slip, 191
Tilton, John, 106
tin/chrome reds, 98
tongs, 18, 48, 62
tools and materials, 16–19
trailing, 51, 82
Trailing Slip for Bisque, 191
trap for waste, 13–14
triaxial blends, 33
troubleshooting, 62
tubs, 16
Tundra Sunset, 61
Turquoise Matte, 180

U

underglazes, 68, 74–75, 79, 193
Unity formula, 22

V

vampire bite marks, 62

Van Guilder Blue Ash, 60–61, 144, 168
Van Zandt, Genevieve, 102–103, 105
Variegated Slate Blue, 176
VC Satin Robin's Egg Blue, 185
VC Satin Stone, 185
vertical forms, dipping, 46
Vickery, Frank, 35, 100, 125, 126

W

wadding, 137, 138, 193
Warm Clear, 186
washes, 76, 193
waste, 13–14
water
 firing and, 132
 in glaze kitchen, 15
wax and wax resist, 46, 48, 78–79
Weber, Julia Claire, 106, 110–111
Wertz Carbon Trap Shino, 167
whisks, 16, 18
Wild West, 60
witness cone, 24, 141
Wolkow Slip, 192
wood firing, 115, 118–121
worktables, 16

Y

Yellow Salt, 54, 59, 141, 168

ABOUT THE AUTHOR

GABRIEL KLINE is a professional potter who has taught ceramics classes for nearly two decades. He is the founder and director of Odyssey ClayWorks, an educational institution affiliated with Highwater Clays—one of the largest clay and ceramic materials companies in the United States. Gabriel serves as the resident artist program director, fostering connections with university programs and up-and-coming artists from around the world. He also directs Odyssey's community volunteer and nonprofit work, including partnerships with various substance abuse and recovery programs as well as Creative Forces, a collaboration between the Departments of Defense and Veterans Affairs, the National Endowment for the Arts, and state arts agencies. His work has been featured in numerous publications, including *The Complete Guide to Mid-Range Glazes*, and the 500 series.